THE WALDO STORY

THE WALDO STORY

The Home of Friendly Merchants

LaDene Morton

The History Press

Published by The History Press
Charleston, SC 29403
www.historypress.net

Cover image courtesy of Dave and Bette Smith.

First published 2012

Manufactured in the United States

ISBN 978.1.60949.472.8

Library of Congress CIP data applied for.

Notice: The information in this book is true and complete to the best of our knowledge. It is offered without guarantee on the part of the author or The History Press. The author and The History Press disclaim all liability in connection with the use of this book.

To all the "Waldonians" who inspired me with their stories

CONTENTS

PREFACE

Kansas City is made up of many communities, each with its own unique character and story. I have been fascinated with such stories all my life. Whenever I am introduced to someplace new, the same questions always confront me. Why this place? What mix of forces caused this place to take root? What events shaped it over the years into what it has become? How has it managed to last when other places like it have faded into history? Who did the hard work that accounts for its success? As a professional in the area of community and economic development for over thirty years, it's been my good fortune to have many opportunities to answer these questions about a wide range of places, many of them in Kansas City. But none has been more intriguing than Waldo, the neighborhood I first moved to when I began my professional life.

I came to Waldo in the early 1980s, into one of the quirky neighborhoods just east of Wornall Road. For eighteen years, I watched Waldo grow and change, all the while managing to keep its small-town charm, even though it was not a town at all. But it wasn't until I had long-since moved out of Waldo and was working on my first book on Kansas City's neighborhoods that I began to answer the questions I had long held on Waldo. That first book, *The Brookside Story: Shops of Every Necessary Character*, covered Waldo's northern neighboring community, a community that seems on its face to be as unlike Waldo as one could imagine. Yet the two places share many influences, and today are embraced and beloved by the same communities. My old curiosities about Waldo were revived. The research on Brookside gave me partial answers to my questions about Waldo, but that wasn't enough. And so the research continued, and as a result, this book was written.

The geographical purist might argue that Waldo does not exist. This is true only so far as it is not now, nor has it ever been, an incorporated municipality. No Jackson County map has ever listed the name "Waldo" in its gazetteer. Yet I can attest to the fact that Waldo very much exists. For most Waldonians (as some locals refer to themselves), Waldo is defined by the boundaries of Gregory Boulevard on the north to Eighty-fifth Street on the south and by Troost Avenue on the east to State Line Road on the west. Waldo is a curious combination of traits—rough around the edges, tinged with a bit of the rural hue, yet very much a part of Kansas City's modern urban life. It is unlike any other part of Kansas City that I know. For me, the answer to the questions about Waldo that confronted me from the beginning is the sum of all the stories included here—the stories of Waldo's businesses, primarily, but also the people who came here, the challenges Waldo has faced and continues to face and how Waldo repeatedly responds to those challenges. My conclusions, however, are my own. I will leave it to the reader to come to his own conclusions about what makes Waldo so, well, "Waldo." After all, if Waldo were that easily defined, it wouldn't be Waldo.

ACKNOWLEDGEMENTS

I was privileged to receive extraordinary assistance in the research of this book from many individuals and organizations, all of whom enthusiastically shared their information and expertise. This research for this book relied heavily on their incredible resources and generosity.

The Waldo Area Business Association's staff and board offered their generous support for this project from its inception and graciously opened their organizational files and archives for research. Information regarding their events, promotions, advertising campaigns and organizational issues came from these archives.

The City of Kansas City Missouri Landmarks Commission provided information on the location of businesses and buildings that might otherwise not have been known. In particular, the Commission's Historic Preservation Office has in its possession photographs taken in 1940 by the Jackson County Tax Assessor's Office. Part of a PWA project, the assessor's office documented all of the buildings standing within Kansas City limits in 1940. These files were obtained after being discarded, so unfortunately many individual pictures were lost. Still, the commission is to be thanked for making this invaluable resource available to myself and to the public at large.

The Missouri Valley Room of the Central Branch of the Kansas City Public Library, widely recognized as Kansas City's most valuable resource for local history, supplied most of the information sourced in newspaper articles, as well as many of the images. Many of the dates and addresses of the Waldo area businesses over the years were gathered from the library's microfilm archives of city directories. A particular thanks goes to staff member Jeremy Drouin who was instrumental in identifying sources of information on Waldo's earliest history.

The Jackson County Historical Society was a critical resource in understanding life in Jackson County when Waldo was little more than a settlement. Special thanks go to the David Jackson, the society's director of archives and education, who provided support even as the society was closed to research during its relocation.

Wilborn & Associates has been capturing images of Kansas City since 1921. Several of their images are included here. In addition, photographer Chris Wilborn and his staff generously shared their archives of images for review to assist in establishing an understanding of changes in Waldo over the years.

The State Historical Society of Missouri's office at the University of Missouri–Kansas City is the repository of the J.C. Nichols Company Scrapbooks, an amazing compilation created by long-time executive secretary of the homes association, Faye Littleton, who, in 1954, began organizing forty years of company history, including some of the images included here, into a compendium of dozens of scrapbooks.

The staff of the jointly managed Alexander Majors Historic House and Museum and the John Wornall House Museum, who provided many materials and unique access to the homes, are to be commended for their work on promoting these unique community historical sites.

The Gillis Center's staff provided a rich resource of material on the history of both the Gillis and Armour Homes, as well as some very personal mementos of their past residents and patrons.

The Waldo Tower Historical Society, committed to the preservation of the Waldo Water Tower at Seventy-fifth Street and Holmes Road, shared both their archival material as well as the work of their current efforts to reclaim this important Waldo landmark.

In addition, I am grateful to the following individuals for their willingness to spend time sharing their stories of the history and life of Waldo. Some of these individuals offered their time and resources specifically for this book; others have, over the years, shared with me the stories of their long association with the Waldo area, stories that greatly helped in my understanding of Waldo's history.

Becky Beck, American Family Insurance
Norman Besheer, Gunter Pest Management
Diane Botwin, Botwin Development
Sam and Mary Gromowsky, Almar Printing
Tom Johnston, Johnston Insurance
Marti Lee, Executive Director, Waldo Area Business Association
Dave and Bette Smith, Dave Smith the Lampmaker
Dr. John J. Turley, Optometrist

Finally, a special acknowledgement and thanks goes to Betty Tillotson. Betty's support and participation is beyond generous. As an author on the history of Waldo, she did not hesitate to share with me her wealth of archival materials, photographic collection, personal remembrances and other resources. Her endorsement of this effort is a great source of personal pride, and I value the friendship I forged with her through our time together. This book would not have been possible without her.

Chapter 1

1840–1860: WHERE THE PATH MAY LEAD

Do not go where the path may lead,
go instead where there is no path and leave a trail.
—Ralph Waldo Emerson

Nothing about the piece of prairie appeared remarkable, or even unusual, in any way. It was flat and treeless, and crossed throughout by a few unremarkable streams. The one thousand acres that Dr. David Waldo purchased in 1841 might have been any one other thousand acres in the area. It was simply chance that led this particular corner to come up for purchase when it did, at just the moment Waldo was looking to buy. Had anyone else bought it, the area obviously would not be known today as "Waldo," a unique corner of Kansas City's urban landscape. But David Waldo's legacy for the area is more than his name.

That legacy begins with his insight about the area, that most clichéd axiom of business—location, location, location. Location was central to David Waldo's objectives. In the short run, he wanted property that was a good location for a farm he needed for breeding and keeping the mules he used in his Santa Fe Trail freighting operation. In the long run, he knew that proximity would continue to make the property an attractive investment, depending on when and where the trails, and the city, grew. Waldo certainly had no plan to start, let alone build, a community that would bear his name. He lacked the ego for that ambition. But in the space of one generation, David Waldo's instinct about the property's location would prove true. His claim would be among the first that would change this corner of the prairie from a wide spot in the road into a trailblazing community that has come to be known as Waldo.

The original property David Waldo purchased—north and east of the current intersection of Seventy-fifth Street and Wornall Road in Kansas City, Missouri—was neither the first nor the largest property he purchased in Jackson County. When he came to western Missouri in the late 1820s, he made Independence, Missouri, his home. Independence was a boomtown then, the latest in a chain of increasingly westward-reaching towns along the Missouri River that serviced the country's western expansion. That burgeoning opportunity had been the allure for Waldo. A man of innumerable talents and broad-ranging vision, he saw instantly in this part of the young state of Missouri a limitless number of enterprising opportunities.

David Waldo was not alone in this foresight. There had been others before him, and there would be more coming. Missouri had been admitted to the union in 1821, and Jackson County formed just five years later (though it would be some years before either completed their modern boundaries). Waldo and others were capitalizing on the boom. Money could be made from the Missouri River traffic that used the area as a jumping-off place for points west. First there had been the explorers and trappers, then the trade with Mexico. By the time Waldo purchased the property just a stone's throw from the border with the western "unorganized territories," the list of travelers had grown to include Methodist missionaries, the Mormon faithful and the first hint of settlers to the far west. Added to the mix was the military, which was establishing a fortification line that would extend far to the south and north and eventually spread throughout the west. There was river traffic and trail traffic, and some even saw far enough into the future to imagine a time when the area would be connected by rail.

All this was in constant motion and hardly predictable. The trailheads had continually moved west—there was no reason to believe they would stop. Each passing year saw new paths emerge, old paths wear into familiar roads and old roads become dotted with settlement. The game was speculation, and the secret to getting wealthy in Jackson County's early days was vision, patience and guts. Those who deciphered the winds of change made money. Those who believed nothing would change lost out. And those with enough capital could hedge their bets in all directions and spread their investments around.

Such was Dr. David Waldo's philosophy, as well as his financial capacity, by this time in his career. As Jackson County continued to annex property,

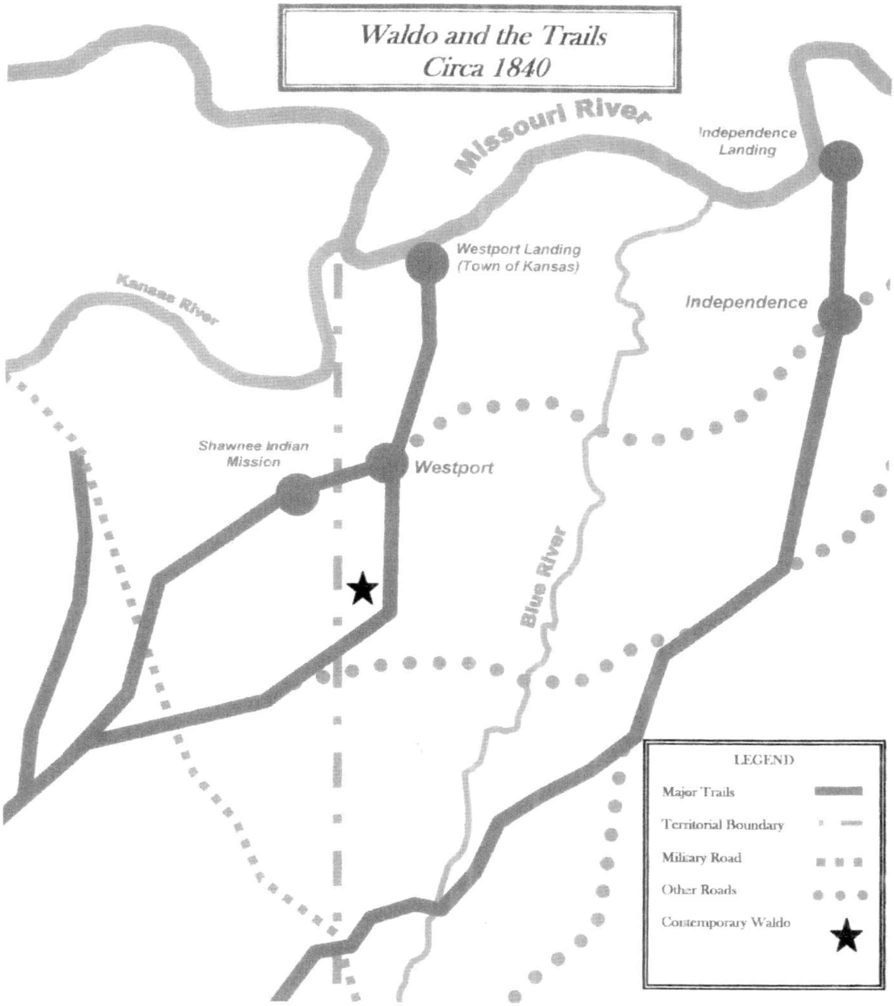

The property David Waldo purchased in 1841 was surrounded by the critical transportation routes of its day. *LaDene Morton.*

Waldo and his contemporaries added to their holdings. The property closest to the territorial wilderness and a fair deal south of the original settlements along the Missouri River was among the last to become available. When it did, it was quickly snatched up by those who saw its potential. But until such time as the property showed its full value, it had to pull its own weight. In Waldo's time, this meant simple agriculture. Like his mule farm, there were many enterprises that required little investment but made ample profit to pay the taxes and put away a tidy sum. Soon this area in west central Jackson County was dotted with hay farms, nut groves and pasture land for livestock, while the owners waited for the opportunities ahead.

The principal opportunity the speculators were waiting for was the inevitable shift in the Santa Fe Trail. The trail serviced trade between the United States and Mexico. Mexico had become free from Spain the same year that Missouri became a state. The trail had started in 1821 in Franklin, a town halfway between Kansas City and St. Louis, just north of the Missouri River. But that hadn't lasted long. Over the first twenty years of the trail's life, the trailhead moved continually west with the advancing civilization. The advantage was always to be the last stop going to Mexico, the first stop coming back. But now the federal government had declared that, for the time being at least, there would be no settlement west of Missouri. The possibility that some place in western Jackson County would be the definitive eastern trailhead seemed real to the land speculators.

Trade with Mexico was a monumental economic force for the area and a considerable part of the national economy as well. The country had been thrown into a depression in 1821 (one that lasted until 1848), but because of trade with Mexico, Missouri did not suffer the same financial decline that the rest of the country experienced. Accounts of the various trading companies of the time reveal a wide swing in year-to-year traffic, but in the first twenty years of the trail, each year saw an average of forty different companies employing a total of one hundred and fifty men moving nearly eighty wagons along the trail, trucking some $130,000 in merchandise. Two years after David Waldo bought his property in west central Jackson County, that rose to $450,000 in goods.

But it would be war, not trade, that would have the next great impact on Waldo's fortunes. The United States' war with Mexico at first seemed a boon for trade, as the Santa Fe Trail was turned into a military supply route. But shortly, the army determined the private teamsters were not up to the demands of "military efficiency." Since most of the supplies the army needed were being shipped to the area by riverboat, the government had them offloaded at Fort Leavenworth, directly into the army's control. The military traffic shifted north, and with a war on, the trade the trail had relied on for so many years all but vanished.

In time, David Waldo and the other speculators would see their opportunity come, though the western Jackson County property would never become the trailhead he might have envisioned. But the men of

Waldo's time were diversified, to say the least. They had partnerships and holdings in all sorts of local businesses, many of which supplied the traders of the Santa Fe Trail and, increasingly, settlers and missionaries bound for the newly opened areas in the Oregon Territory. When gold was discovered in California in 1849, there was a whole new market for their supplies. By then, the floodgates of opportunity in the West were wide open. Westport had replaced Independence as the center of trail activity. Much of David Waldo's property was just a few miles south of there, convenient to the action. It wasn't the last jumping-off place, but it was close enough. And the seeds of enterprise planted in Waldo's property along the frontier's border would grow roots that would run deep and last long.

Dr. David Waldo—A Brief Biography

David Waldo was born April 3, 1802, in Clarksburg, West Virginia, on authority of an article written by his grandson, Waldo Douglas Sloan, for the Jackson County Historical Society in 1968. Other sources have attributed Waldo's birthplace to Virginia. Whatever his birthplace, Waldo only spent his first eighteen years outside Missouri. In 1820, he moved to Gasconade County. Why he chose Gasconade isn't known, but in hindsight, it is easy to see what may have attracted him to the place. Still, Waldo displayed remarkable insight, particularly for his young years. Insight would be a distinguishing characteristic for him throughout his life.

Missouri was about to be designated a state then, and Gasconade was one of the first counties established when that happened. The Missouri River, with all its riverboat traffic moving goods to and from St. Louis, was the county's northern border. Its interior was filled with woodlands ripe for the cutting, and the Gasconade River made it easy to move the wood to trade. Young David Waldo made what some considered later a small fortune off the timber, helped in part by his brothers who had joined him in Missouri. The money he made was certainly sufficient to invest in his future, to position himself for more and better opportunities. This, too, would be a lifelong trait.

In 1821, Waldo took his earnings and traveled to Lexington, Kentucky, to attend medical school at Transylvania College. Academic requirements being considerably less than present-day, Waldo earned his medical

The only known portrait of Dr. David Waldo, circa 1860. *Jackson County (MO) Historical Society Archives.*

degree in one year and returned to Gasconade as Dr. David Waldo. Now he had a profession. He also had an instinct for civic interests, another recurring attribute. As a man of education now, he quickly became involved in the local business and political communities. In a short time, he held a number of influential and strategic positions—postmaster, county assessor, county treasurer, circuit court clerk, justice of the peace and deputy sheriff, among them. In his spare time, he practiced medicine. One account of this period recounts that Waldo became known locally as "governor of Gasconade." He accomplished all this by the age of twenty-six.

He could have easily and successfully lived out the rest of his life in Gasconade. But he wouldn't have been content. The same instinct for budding opportunity that had first drawn him to Missouri drew his attention farther and farther west, as the years went by. In 1828, at the invitation of a friend and business acquaintance, Waldo traveled up river to Independence, Missouri. David Waldo's host, Samuel C. Owens, was himself already making a fortune in the Santa Fe trade, but Owens's view of the world was larger than Missouri. He shipped merchandise not just between Mexico and Missouri, but also all the way to the industrial east. He is considered by some to be the "first citizen" of Independence. He believed that Independence would be the next, and perhaps last, great eastern trail station. Owens was in the business of convincing others that this was so. His success was dependent on it, as he was heavily invested in the area. He recognized that a man of David Waldo's ingenuity and enterprise would be a welcome asset to the area.

David Waldo, interested as he was in new opportunities, was easily persuaded by Owens. He moved to Independence and began buying property around Jackson County. He made his home in Independence, but there was scarcely a township in Jackson County where David Waldo did not own land. Over the course of his life, there would be many purchases and sales of property. But the property some four miles south of Westport would be among his largest contiguous holdings and where he put the most effort.

Samuel Owens also enticed Waldo into traveling with him on a trade expedition to Santa Fe, then still a part of Mexico. For a man of Waldo's inquisitive nature and entrepreneurial leanings, the invitation would have seemed the chance of his young life. The trip proved as much adventure as opportunity. Their first journey south introduced Waldo to some of the most important and colorful characters of the early days of the frontier. Some are lesser known but critical in their influence, such as Ceran St. Vrain, one of the leading fur traders of the day, based in St. Louis. On that first trip, Waldo and St. Vrain formed a partnership for a freighting expedition. That partnership made St. Vrain and Waldo a nice profit.

By the next year, Waldo had enlisted brother William to leave Gasconade County and join him again, this time shipping goods in from St. Louis. The Waldo brothers would lead the train to Santa Fe themselves. They took seventy men and thirty-seven wagons. Their captain was Charles Bent, who, with Bent's brother William and St. Vrain, had established Bent's Fort in modern-day southeast Colorado. Bent was another major figure of the West in those days. In his future, Charles Bent would be named the first governor of territorial New Mexico.

In these and various other partnerships, Waldo and his partners would hire trappers, teamsters and guides, among them the legendary Kit Carson and his brother Moses. Also during this period, Waldo became friends with Josiah Gregg, whose 1844 publication on the Santa Fe Trail, *The Commerce of the Prairies*, was so widely circulated that it became the most influential resource for promoting westward expansion. In the book, Gregg attributes David Waldo as a primary source of true and critical information on trade with Mexico.

From his late twenties to his mid-forties, David Waldo led an exhilarating life. When at home in Independence, he was an active and prominent citizen, thoroughly well-respected and sought-after as a business partner. With his professional degree and the reputation of his considerable civic history in Gasconade, the citizenry of Independence considered him among its most important and educated residents.

On the trail, he had another persona altogether. There, Waldo was part teamster, part fighter. By doing the work himself, Waldo learned what sold and what didn't, and he learned how to organize a successful convoy of men and goods. He trucked household goods to Mexico and brought back Mexico's resources in the form of furs, minerals and livestock, particularly mules. He encountered trouble with Indians almost from the start. On its first trip with Bent, the Waldo party was attacked shortly after crossing into government territory. One of the teamsters was killed, though the goods had been what they were after. For the next month on the trail, the harassment continued, and Waldo and Bent repeatedly had to fight off their attackers. Through the years, they are said to have both earned reputations as fearless men who never backed down from a fight.

In Mexico, Waldo had yet another reputation. There, in his dealings with other traders, he was clever and strategic. Bargains were struck at the Mexican end of the trail, as well as up north. Here, too, his reputation as a fair man made him a popular business partner. But there was a political climate to consider in Mexico. So David Waldo became a Mexican citizen, on paper at least. It afforded him a few advantages, not the least of which was his apparent commitment to both ends of the trail. He also practiced medicine a bit in Mexico and is considered to have been the first doctor to practice in Taos. In Santa Fe, he opened stores and banks. He was a solid member of the Santa Fe and Taos communities.

In the mid-1830s, about midway into the preeminent years of David Waldo's career, internal conflicts between the Mexican government and its provinces began to make freighting along the Santa Fe Trail increasingly dangerous. The uncertainty along the trail caused David Waldo to focus his attentions on other aspects of his growing business, in particular on his Jackson County land holdings. In 1841, David Waldo purchased the land that is today part of the Waldo community. The greatest contiguous acreage constitutes much of what today lies between Wornall Road and Troost Avenue, north of Seventy-fifth Street. At one thousand acres, it was the largest of Waldo's holdings throughout Jackson County. He built a house and barn and convinced another brother, Lawrence, to manage his Mexican mules on the farm. Waldo also planted a grove of walnut trees that were for many years the only cluster of trees on the open prairie. It was no doubt a nice little farm, but David Waldo was no farmer, and his interests in it were purely to support his other operations. As it turned out, his brother Lawrence shared David's disdain for farming and his love of adventure. Shortly after taking over the mule operation, Lawrence Waldo turned it over to his wife so that he could join brothers David and William in the freight operation business.

His brothers proved more than capable as freighters, so when the United States went to war with Mexico in 1846, David Waldo was able to be a part of the fight. By this time, he was forty-four years old and no longer a young man, but he felt compelled to join in. After all, he was a patriot with strong business interests at both ends of the conflict. The United States Army recognized the value of Waldo's personal experiences in Mexico. He was made a captain in the Missouri Mounted Volunteers. On June 22, 1846, Waldo's regiment departed from Fort Leavenworth under the command of Colonel Alexander Doniphan as part of the famed "Kearney's Army of the West." The soldiers reached Santa Fe unscathed. Upon arrival in Santa Fe, the U.S. Army declared New Mexico to be a territory, and Waldo was on hand to witness his old friend Charlie Bent sworn in as the territory's first governor. In the two years of the war, David Waldo saw only one major conflict, in which his reputation as a fearless fighter was reaffirmed. The writer and historian Rudolph Umland attributed Waldo with this famous quote made during that battle, which seems to sum up both Waldo's fearlessness and pragmatism: "Shoot low! Shoot low, boys! If you break one man's leg, it will take two men to carry him off!"

When the war with Mexico ended in 1848, David Waldo moved dramatically away from the life he had lived for so long. He kept his trade business but favored a less speculative government contract, under the name Waldo & Company, to ship supplies for the army. The world was changing, and adventure had taken its toll. Only four months after his appointment as governor, Waldo's friend Charlie Bent was ambushed in his home in New Mexico and murdered by rebels. Tragically, a few days later, Waldo's brother Lawrence was killed in a fight with Mexican revolutionists over the caravan he was leading. Now Waldo had Lawrence's young family who needed his financial support.

Shortly thereafter, Waldo had his own family to support. On March 27, 1849, at the age of forty-seven, David Waldo married for the first time in his life. The bride was Eliza Norris of Independence, twenty years his junior, and the daughter of a prominent local family. In a few short years, the Waldos were the parents of five children. The change seems to have domesticated David Waldo. Visitors to their house recount the elegant decorations in their home at what is today 1018 West Waldo Avenue in Independence, Missouri. In those years, Waldo led a gentrified life. He read and translated Spanish, Greek and Latin (all self-taught). He remained current on all events and politics of the day and was a favorite of Independence society, always with something to offer any conversation. He was well known to drive about town in a fine carriage pulled by two black mules, and Waldo proudly declared himself a "mule man" after all his days on the Santa Fe Trail. He remained active in business, mostly managing his assets and dabbling in a little trade, and he expanded his government contract work the same year as his marriage. Through a partnership that included Kansas City founding father William McCoy, the stagecoaches of Waldo, Hall & Company carried passengers and mail deliveries across the Indian territories between 1850 and 1854.

The Civil War years took their toll on David Waldo. Like many of his Missouri contemporaries, he was that curious combination of a slaveholder who seemed to have Unionist sympathies. As a result, he was neither side's friend, and the conflicts associated with both the guerilla actions of the "border war" and the subsequent Battle of Westport left much of his property decimated. After the war, his behavior was variously described as "eccentric" and "depressed." He was inclined to fits of insomnia, of disorientation and memory loss, and he may have suffered from dementia. In the late 1860s, he was admitted to an asylum. After years of taking morphine to help him sleep, he died of an overdose of the opiate in 1878, at the age of seventy-six.

His unfortunate end did not diminish David Waldo's reputation in the community, nor did it lessen the unending affections of his family. Years later, writing for the Jackson County Historical Society, his grandson Waldo Douglas Sloan recounted how his mother, Lula Waldo Sloan, remembered her father.

> *His mental faculties were marked by great strength, breadth and quickness; his heart, like his intellect, was large, vivid and keenly sensitive; his imagination far-reaching and brilliant. Over these splendid powers there reigned a will so strong that he could command his strongest emotions to remain unseen in the secret recesses of his soul and allow himself to execute his business enterprises without their interferences. He was a constant reader, genial and social, and of sunny nature. A grand, noble man; an earnest Christian.*

Waldo's most tangible legacy came many years later as the community that formed from his early investments south of Westport took his name as its own. But his real legacy may be that so many of his enduring and endearing qualities—an entrepreneurial spirit, a keen instinct for opportunity and a commitment to community—came to be values that would form and preserve the Waldo community in the coming years.

The House that Majors Built

Unquestionably, Alexander Majors is among the most famous people ever to call the Waldo area home, and in terms of his impact on the history of the American West, he is likely the most important. And although his time in the Waldo area was relatively short, the trail business operated off his property (now at 8201 State Line Road) is the last remaining vestige of the original enterprises that forever established Waldo as a community of commerce.

Born in 1814, Alexander Majors's family moved to Lafayette County, Missouri from Kentucky when he was only five. His father Benjamin came west, looking to establish a new farm in a place that offered more prosperity. Majors's mother, Laurania, was injured on the trip. It was a minor fall that happened just west of St. Louis, but she never fully recovered and died some months later. The loss affected young Alexander greatly, resulting in his lifelong devotion to her memory and his determination to uphold her values of hard work and a proper Christian bearing in everything he did.

Farming for a young man raising three small children alone was a hardscrabble life, and the elder Majors barely made enough to keep the farm running. No wonder, then, that in 1827, Benjamin Majors jumped at a chance to go fortune hunting. He joined a party in search of a silver deposit in the Rocky Mountains and left his children in the care of others. The West was still largely unexplored, and almost completely devoid of way stations or supply depots for the adventurer. Though the silver ore was found, the value of the mine proved minimal. But when his father returned to the farm, his tales of the journey enthralled young Alexander, and formed the young boy's first impressions of the opportunities that the western frontier held for a man willing to take a risk.

When Alexander turned twenty-one, he married Katherine Stalcup. Together, the young couple looked to a farming life as Majors's father had done. As their family grew, however, Majors saw his prospects shrink. He began to scout around for other opportunities. In his later years, he wrote, "[I]t occurred to me there was nothing I was so well adapted for by my past experience as the freighting business that was then being conducted between Independence, Missouri, and Santa Fe, New Mexico, a distance of eight hundred miles."

Majors picked a good time to enter the freighting business. He made his first venture in August 1848. The war with Mexico had passed, and the

Alexander Majors at the height of his professional career, circa 1860. *Alexander Majors Historical Trust.*

military presence in the West made the trip less risky. The growing list of military outposts added the federal government to the long list of lucrative freight customers. Majors quickly proved adept as a freight operator. His first trip, starting late in the season as it did, should have faced more problems with weather and lack of grass for the grazing livestock. Yet not only did he prevail, but he made the round trip in a record time for ox teams (as opposed to mules)—just ninety-two days. The solid reputation of Alexander Majors had begun to solidify.

That reputation was further enhanced by his work ethic. He created a code of conduct for his teamsters, or as the men themselves referred to them, Majors's "iron-clad rules." Each employee Majors hired signed his name to the following: "While I am in the employ of A. Majors, I agree not to use profane language, not to get drunk, not to gamble, not to treat animals cruelly and not to do anything else that is incompatible with the conduct of a gentleman. And I agree, if I violate any of the above conditions, to accept my discharge without any pay for my services."

Later, when the Civil War broke out in 1861, Majors would add to his code a statement of allegiance to the government of the United States. Majors never had occasion to fire a single employee for violation of his code. And throughout his career, he would consistently count this adherence to good conduct and moral behavior as the single greatest contribution to his success.

For the next seven years, Majors continued to enjoy increasing success in the freighting business, enhanced in turns by the opening of the Oregon Territory for settlement in 1848, the rush to the California gold fields in 1849 and the expansion of military forts in the west through the 1850s. In 1855, Alexander Majors joined forces with two earlier business acquaintances from his days in Lafayette County to create the firm of

Russell, Majors and Waddell, one of the West's preeminent freighting companies. It was a profitable venture that quickly grew. Soon they employed more than four thousand men and owned 3,500 wagons and nearly forty thousand oxen. One of those he hired was an eleven-year-old William Cody. The boy's mother had come to Majors, pleading with him to give Cody work after his father died and left the family destitute. Majors and Cody formed a life-long friendship.

With his newfound prosperity, Majors purchased the property on the state line in 1856 and started the construction of a fine house. The house would have a long life, but most of it was without Majors. Two years later, the contract system with the army had changed. Supplies were chiefly coming out of Fort Leavenworth, and Majors saw opportunities farther north. His first wife had died, and he had remarried. He moved his family to Nebraska City, Nebraska, to oversee the firm's contract for shipments to Utah. The state line property was given to his daughter Rebecca, by then the young wife of Majors's first wagon master, Samuel Poteet.

The firm of Russell, Majors and Waddell is credited with the creation of the Pony Express, a brief but colorful chapter in American history. Operating as the Central Overland California and Pikes Peak Express Company, the Pony Express began in April 1860 and ran between St. Joseph, Missouri, and Sacramento, California. The venture lasted only eighteen months. First, it was merely unprofitable, but soon it was made obsolete by the telegraph and the ever increasing advances west. Russell, Majors and Waddell, facing changing times and furtively trying to keep up with the demands of contracts, overextended their capacity. The firm simply borrowed too much. When Majors's partner William Russell found himself embroiled in a national financial scandal involving closed-door dealings with the U.S. Department of the Interior, the firm's already concerned investors lost all confidence. Russell, Majors and Waddell effectively closed its doors in 1862.

After that, the story of Alexander Majors clouds over. His second marriage had brought him a second family, but that marriage fell apart for unknown reasons. There are historical reports that his wife and at least one child were admitted to the Jackson County Poor Farm under assumed names, to avoid the shame. His children with his first wife, Katherine—those that had survived childhood—were now adults on their own. All alone now, Majors continued in business, but he left Nebraska and drifted around the West. He spent time in Salt Lake City, where he worked in support of the Union Pacific Railroad's drive west and was witness to

Majors (center) at the time of the publication of his memoir, surrounded by his former teamsters "Pony Bob" Haslam (standing left), John B. Colton (seated left), Buffalo Bill Cody (seated right) and his publisher, Prentiss Ingram (standing right). *Alexander Majors Historical Trust.*

the driving of the "golden spike" at Promontory Summit when the first transcontinental railroad was completed in 1869. He is known to have lived for a time in Denver, where his old friend Buffalo Bill Cody found him working on his memoirs. Cody arranged to have the book published in 1893 by Rand McNally. Today, Majors's *Seventy Years on the Frontier* continues to stand as one of the great narrative accounts of the early years of the frontier West. Majors died in January 1900 in Chicago. The *New York Times* reported the famous man's death. In its obituary, the paper recounted that Majors was in Chicago visiting an old friend from his mining days, trying to get "an invention on the market." His body was returned to Kansas City, where he is buried in Union Cemetery alongside his first wife.

Back in Kansas City, the house that Majors built was still standing. In 1904, it was sold by Majors's heirs to Mr. and Mrs. A. Louis Ruhl, who built an addition to the house. Mrs. Ruhl owned the house until 1924. By that time, the surge of residential growth had spread sufficiently southward to make the property attractive for development. Much of the original acreage was platted and subdivided for a residential development called Cresthill Acres. To accommodate the new residents' needs, the Majors house was turned into a school that also doubled as a community meetinghouse. Continued growth prompted a plan four years later to demolish the old house and build a new school building. The house itself thwarted that plan. With its sturdy timber framing and iron nails, the demolition contractor deemed the house too costly to tear down for the quoted price. The school was built elsewhere, and the Majors home was left standing but abandoned.

The Alexander Majors House, still occupied by members of his family, circa 1860. *Alexander Majors Historical Trust.*

In 1930, Louisa Johnston, Alexander Majors's great-granddaughter, came to view her ancestral home and found it in a decrepit state. The brick chimneys were crumbling, the hardware had been stripped from its doors and every one of its forty-six windows was broken. "I decided if the house was to be saved, I must buy it," she later said. She paid three thousand dollars for the property. Johnston began work on the house in 1932, but she had only her public school teacher's salary to bankroll the effort. She worked diligently for the next forty years to restore the house, with the ultimate goal of turning the property into a memorial to her ancestor and his place in history. There were glimmers of hope over those years. In 1945, then senator Harry Truman introduced a bill that would have provided for the purchase and maintenance of the home, but the bill did not pass the House of Representatives. Johnston continued her campaign, writing literally hundreds of letters to elected officials, private businesses, developers and civic organizations—anyone she thought might help. The response was invariably good wishes for her efforts, but no money. Aided by the Russell-Majors-Waddell National Historic Association, the house's one good stroke of fortune was to be listed on the Register of National Historic Sites in 1970.

Then, in 1976, the City of Kansas City adopted a plan for development between Ward Parkway and State Line Road, from Seventy-ninth to Eighty-fifth Streets. That plan provided for a six-acre park surrounding the Majors home. The plan for the park was contingent upon agreements between the Russell-Majors-Waddell Association (who wanted to purchase the home), other corporations and private developers with property interests in the area and grant funds from the U.S. Department of the Interior. Despite the plan, the project failed to get off the ground for nearly ten years. Louisa Johnston died in 1979, leaving the house to Terry W. Chapman, who had served as restoration architect for the house. The structural work was completed in 1983, and the following year, the house was the subject of the Kansas City Symphony's annual Designer Showcase project, which provided some of the interior finishes.

The house was finally opened to the public in 1984 as the Alexander Majors House Museum. It has remained open to the public ever since for tours and events. In 2010, the Majors House merged its operations with those of the John Wornall House and Museum at Sixty-first Street and Wornall Road, strengthening the historic legacy of the area and providing a more certain future for Alexander Majors's grand home on the edge of the frontier.

Other Places, Other Names

History can be fickle when it comes to what is remembered and what is forgotten. Notoriety does not always come to the influential, and still others who deserve it are often left behind. When Waldo was still just a wide spot in the road—if that—there were other communities in the area that were thriving. Some still exist, though like Waldo, they bear little resemblance to their early beginnings. Others were bypassed by new routes or missed out on a chance to be linked by rail or were swallowed up by growth.

Dallas

Waldo's closest neighbor was the town of Dallas, about three miles to the south and west. That Dallas existed at all was thanks to the Fitzhugh Mill, built in 1832 on the banks of Indian Creek. The spot was on the Santa Fe Trail, and its cool grove and natural waterfall were an inviting rest stop for travelers after their first day's ride south from Westport. Brothers Jonathan and George Fitzhugh milled corn and wheat and sold much of

The mill once operated by Stubbin Watts near 103rd Street and State Line Road stood until the 1940s. Today, the foundation remains, and the surrounding area is a park. This photo shows the mill as it appeared in a 1927 Jackson County planning report. *LaDene Morton.*

the flour to the freighters and travelers. Over the next twenty years, the mill continued to serve the trail traffic, though the mill itself would change hands, eventually purchased by Anthony Watts. Under this ownership, the mill, and the place once known as Dallas, became known as Watts Mill. The famous Jim Bridger, legendary mountain man and a close friend of Watts's, bought property to farm on the south side of the creek. He lived there until his death in 1881. The mill was still operating when it celebrated its centennial, but it closed a few years later in 1939, no longer able to compete with Kansas City's more modern mills. During World War II, the building's iron was sold for scrap to support the war effort. The building was razed in 1949. When Kroh Realty purchased the property in the 1970s, they donated the mill site to the city, and today it is open to the public as a park. The last building associated with the town of Dallas was torn down in 1992. Today, the mill's foundation is still visible from a walking trail that follows Indian Creek. The adjacent shopping district has long adopted the name "Watts Mill."

New Santa Fe

The little town of New Santa Fe emerged from homesteads established around 1833 near present-day Minor Drive between Wornall and State Line Roads. About four miles farther south than Dallas on the Santa Fe Trail, New Santa Fe thrived for a short time as a way station, with the extra advantage of being at the convergence of the trails leading from both Westport and Independence. But unlike Dallas—or Waldo, for that matter—New Santa Fe was incorporated as a town, established in 1852. The records of the Jackson County Historical Society tell of a thriving place in its day, with a population of five hundred, served by two general stores, an inn, a post office, a doctor and a saloon that straddled the state line and served as a public room for the transaction of business. Its strategic location proved to be a disadvantage during the years leading up to the Civil War. Much of New Santa Fe was burned in the mid-1850s during the border conflict. Following the Battle of Westport, the Confederate forces camped there briefly as they fled south. But ultimately, it was the railroad—or lack of it—that sealed the town's fate. When it failed to connect to any of the new rails being built in the area in the 1880s, New Santa Fe slowly faded from existence. All that remains today is the New Santa Fe Cemetery, just south of the original town site. Today, the cemetery is under the care of the New Santa Fe Cemetery Association. A separate organization, the Historical Society of New Santa Fe, helps promote the area's unique heritage.

Dodson

Perhaps no other community born in those early days has as direct a connection to Waldo as Dodson. Dodson's experience was the opposite of New Santa Fe. It sprung from the Missouri Pacific's decision in the 1880s to run its tracks near the Blue River, near the current intersection of Eighty-fifth Street and Prospect Avenue. Dodson took its name from Billy Dodson, an area property owner. When an interurban rail line was developed in the 1880s, the Dodson Line provided a connection for folks

The community of Dodson was the link between the Missouri Pacific Railroad and the freight service that ran to Waldo. This photo shows Dodson as it appeared in a 1927 Jackson County planning report. *LaDene Morton.*

in the rural areas of the county coming in to take advantage of the city attractions and conveniences they needed. Soon, a little community grew near the convergence of the two rail lines. Farmers shipped produce and livestock on the line into the city's markets and slaughterhouses. Starting in the 1920s, Dodson became the final stop on the streetcar line as the city grew southward and was still a stop on the line when operation ceased in 1957. Today, Dodson continues as one of the city's oldest and most thriving industrial parks, with the railroad still its lifeline.

While David Waldo is the man whose name was given to the Waldo area, it certainly wasn't known as Waldo in his time. It would largely be due to the efforts of his son, David Waldo Jr., who popularized the name. Waldo the elder owned many properties in the area, but after his passing, his heirs continued to own those properties for many years. The junior Waldo first used the name "Waldo" in the 1890s when he began developing some of his father's original property under the company he formed, the Waldo Land & Investment Company. The largest tract he called "Waldo Park," an area between Seventy-first and Seventy-fifth Streets, Wornall Road to Holmes Road, which for a brief time included a horse track known as the Waldo Race Track.

Early on, Seventy-first Street was listed on some maps as Waldo Lane, securing forever what has come to be considered as Waldo's northern boundary. But that name faded as the city grew. It wouldn't be until 1930 that Seventy-first Street took the name "Gregory Boulevard." In 1853, William Gregory was Kansas City's first elected mayor, defeating another recognizable name, Dr. Benoist Troost, by just nine votes out of sixty-three registered voters. Gregory only served for ten months, but during that time, he appointed the city's first administrators—a city treasurer, tax collector and city attorney among them—and helped write the city charter. Ironically, it was that charter that forced him from office, for the charter required the mayor to be a resident of the city's incorporated area. Gregory lived just east of the city, on Locust Street. Gregory resigned, but he continued to serve as a city alderman. In 1930, a resident called attention to the fact that, unlike other founding fathers, the city had never recognized its first mayor by naming a street after him. Through a resolution of the Park Board, William Gregory was finally so honored.

Waldo's other main thoroughfare, Wornall Road, was named for John Bristow Wornall, who owned a great deal of property just north of Waldo. The Wornall home, a central site during the Battle of Westport, still stands at Sixty-first Street and Wornall Road, and it is open to the public as a museum. Over the years, the Wornall family has owned large tracts of property extending south and west from the homestead.

Other famous names have been associated with Waldo's early years, including:

Boone

Both Daniel Morgan Boone (namesake son of the famous frontiersman) and his sons Napoleon and Morgan owned property at the south end of present-day Waldo. Napoleon's acreage extended to include the northeast corner of today's intersection of Eighty-fifth Street and Wornall Road.

Armour

The name Armour has been synonymous with meat packing since the mid-nineteenth century. At one time, the Armour family owned a significant piece of property spanning Wornall Road just south of present-day Brookside (Sixty-third Street), and extending west into Kansas. The property was used as a Hereford farm. The Nichols Company eventually purchased much of that property for the development of residential areas such as Romanelli Gardens and Armour Hills.

Mockbee

The Mockbee family name has been carried down through history most notably because their farm site at Seventy-eight Street and Holmes Road was the site of an artillery battle during the Battle of the Blue, one of the key engagements just prior to the Battle of Westport. Though that farmstead is long gone, the Mockbee family continued to own much of the property east of Wornall Road into the twentieth century.

Chapter 2

1860–1900: BEGINNING A NEW LIFE

It is easy to see that, under the sharp discipline of civil war, the nation is beginning a new life.
—Abraham Lincoln

The opening of the West had brought great prosperity to the state of Missouri and to that settlement at the confluence of the Kaw and the great Missouri River still known in 1860 as the "City of Kansas." Local fortunes had been made speculating in the nation's expansion. Whatever the intrepid American soul needed to secure each foothold of the push westward—trade goods, emigrants, soldiers—Missouri and Jackson County had been more than happy to oblige.

Starting in the mid-1850s, the flow of emigration had widened yet again. There were still the now familiar assortment of miners, missionaries and farmers heading out west, but there were others whose destinations were closer and whose purposes were political. On the heels of the 1854 Kansas-Nebraska Act, members of the Massachusetts Emigrant Aid Company traveled to the Kansas Territory to sway the coming vote to stand as a free or slave state upon its imminent admission to the Union. The government had done its part when it opened the lands from the border to two hundred miles west. When the abolitionists arrived, proslavery forces soon joined the match. It was a rush to claim more than mere land. At stake was the course of the nation, the rights of the states against the right of free men. But though the stakes were

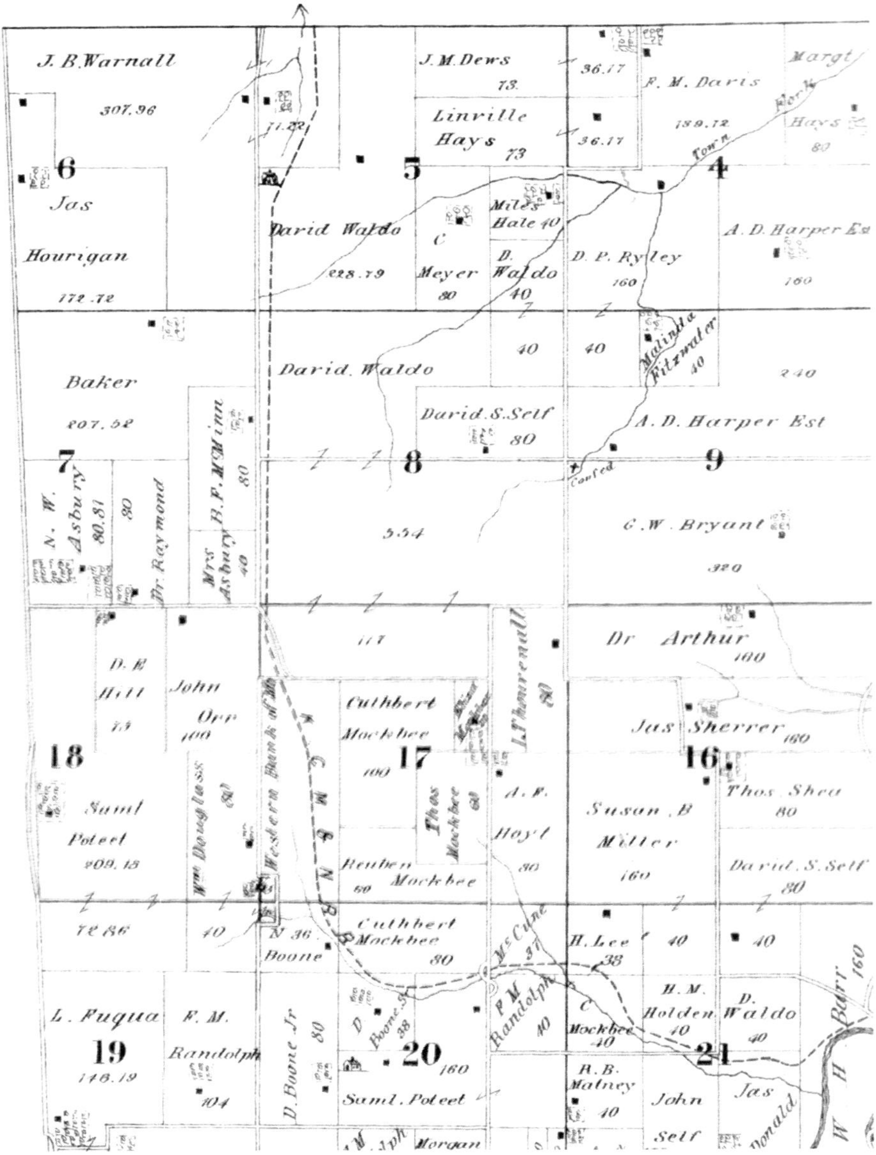

The extent of David Waldo's holdings in the area is shown in this 1878 atlas of Jackson County. *Jackson County (MO) Historical Society Archives.*

far-reaching, the battle that was about to begin would remain a very personal one for those who fought along the border.

The resulting period of protracted brutality and hardship ran the full length of the territorial border. Before the Civil War would officially start in April 1861, virtually every property owner within those two hundred miles of the Missouri–Kansas border suffered. Within months of the war's end, what became known as the Battle of Westport laid waste to much of everything south of Brush Creek. In between, the war brought trade to a near stop for four long years, stripping away the livelihood of most everyone in Jackson County.

After the war, Lincoln's vision that through war the nation was "beginning a new life" proved true, and nowhere was that more apparent than in the City of Kansas. Though divisions remained, city fathers who had been on opposite sides during the conflict understood the value of partnership in promoting the city's advantages to the world. They set their sights increasingly on more ambitious—and some said far-fetched—goals for the city, the greatest of which would be the first bridge across the Missouri River, for a railroad that could put Kansas City at the crossroads of every important commercial venture in the land for generations to come.

There were other aspects of this "new life" that would accompany the prosperity Kansas City witnessed in the 1870s and '80s. It was not, of course, a prosperity shared by all. The railroads made the slaughterhouse trade the most important part of the local economy. The livestock pens, the rail yards and the meat packing plants were filthy, smelly, dangerous places to work. While some made fortunes, others with too little money to begin with were spending their pay at the proliferation of sporting houses, gambling halls and saloons that accounted for much of the new construction along the city's spreading streets. Families were abandoned, children orphaned and lives ruined, and only the charity of the families who were making fortunes off the new prosperity kept even more from destitution.

The growth in population, the ability of those who could to move farther and farther from the squalor and the crime of a boomtown kept the city's limits moving ever south and eastward. Just before the dawn of a new century, the City of Kansas City was finally successful in annexing the town of Westport, a place that had once been its larger and more prosperous sibling. In the years to come, Waldo's connection to Westport—the rail—would prove to be its link to its own boom years.

FROM BORDER TO BATTLE—THE CIVIL WAR AND WALDO

However noble the cause, the war between the Union and the Confederacy was brutal on both sides of the Mason-Dixon line. It was no less brutal on both sides of the Missouri-Kansas border. When the Massachusetts Emigrant Aid Company sponsored some two hundred emigrants for relocation in Lawrence, Kansas, in 1854, the conflict was officially engaged. For the next four years, the abolitionist "Free Staters" in Kansas and "Border Ruffian" proslavery forces in Missouri would battle with both wits and guns. The battle of wits was a series of brinksmanship moves to establish a constitution for the soon-to-be new State of Kansas. Territorial conventions were held variously by both sides in an assortment of northeast Kansas settlements. Accordingly, each side established a series of temporary territorial capitals. For a short time, the proslavery interests even established their capital as near as the Shawnee Indian Mission in present-day Fairway, Kansas.

The battle of guns was the sum of the skirmishes known as "The Border Conflict." Between 1855 and 1859, guerrilla bands from Missouri instigated a series of raids in northeast Kansas. As they moved across the border, they burned, pillaged and, in some cases, murdered the opposition. In the first sacking of Lawrence, Kansas, in 1856, the guerillas were in collaboration with the Douglas County sheriff. On the side of the free-state interests, the notorious John Brown retaliated with his own brand of violence, hacking to death nonslaveholder Southern sympathizers in Pottawatomie, Kansas, that same year.

While these early battles may have been in Kansas, life just across the border in Missouri would have been just as horrific. Local loyalties were divided. There were likely as many of Kansas City's prominent citizens who supported the antislavery forces as there were for the proslavery side. The Border Ruffians were known to conscript men and supplies as needed when they took off on their raids, and they didn't seem to care which side of the border they stole from. David Waldo, Alexander Majors and their fellow landholders along the border were already struggling to keep their properties on a paying basis. Such constant uncertainty would not have helped. To make matters worse, capital was tight for the freighting business. No sane investor wanted to gamble on an expedition that led directly into "Bleeding Kansas."

Trade with Mexico, along with any traffic to the far West, all but dried up when the Civil War officially broke out in 1861. The demand on the government's resources meant the loss of a primary source of business for Waldo and the other freighters. Worse still, once the conflict was formally engaged, the Free Staters who had suffered so much before the war now saw the opportunity for retaliation. They had the support of any federal troops in the area. The troops provided unofficial sanction to vigilante raids and, in some cases, provided direct support. In his account of the life of David Waldo, Rudolph Umland notes that the doctor's enterprises suffered heavily during the war years and that "marauding bands of guerillas drove off his horses, destroyed his fences, burned his buildings" to such an extent that the war is considered by some historians to be one of the major contributors to David Waldo's later mental decline. And when the federal government issued General Order No. 11 in 1863, forcing farmers in rural Jackson County to leave their property regardless of their loyalties, the Waldo area farmers would certainly have been among those exiled. In many cases, the buildings on the seized properties were burned to the ground, but only after supplies and livestock were confiscated.

Far to the east, forces were conspiring to bring the terror of full-fledged battle to Missouri. The tide had shifted against the Confederacy by 1863. The South needed victories, supplies and a shift in public opinion. All this, the Confederate generals believed, could be accomplished by turning their energies toward Missouri. General Sterling Price was commanded to take St. Louis and its wealth of supplies. Should that prove too heavily defended, then the strategy was to capture the state capitol, Jefferson City, and continue as far west as possible, with the Indian Territory in the West the end game.

Price invaded Missouri from northeastern Arkansas in mid-September, equipped with a wagon train that he intended to fill with the spoils of war so as to help supply the Confederacy. He never reached St. Louis, nor did he reach Jefferson City, for that matter. In both cases, Price's forces made it to within a few miles of his destination—Pilot Knob and Booneville, respectively—before he clashed with Union troops and failed to make ground. His only success was to inflict damage on the enemy and to add stores to his supply train, which by now was slowing down his westward progress. At Sedalia and Lexington, Price finally scored victories, though he could not secure either town for long. But by now, the Union army had seen the invaders up close and fully knew Price's capacity and his

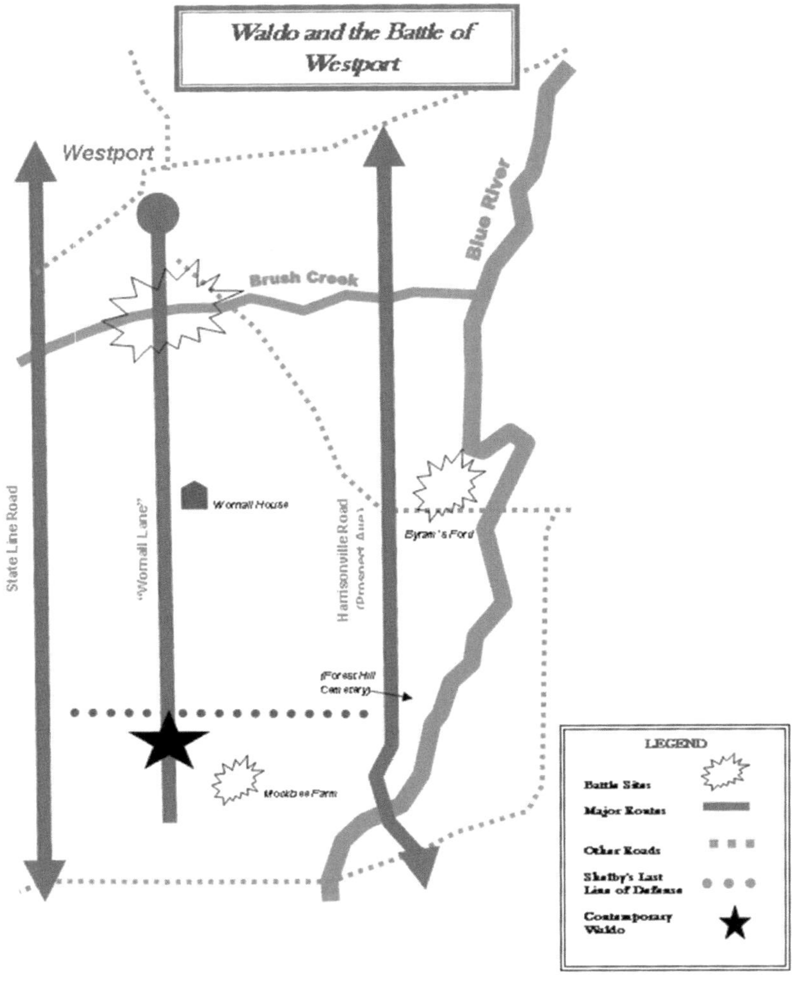

While Waldo was still in its formative state, the Battle of Westport in 1864 would have been a significant site of military action. *LaDene Morton.*

weaknesses. What they saw were battle-weary, laden-down soldiers and wagons. Yet onward the Confederate troops came. On October 21, 1863, they crossed the Little Blue River and took Independence, the seat of Jackson County. Now Price set his sights on the next prize—Westport.

Word of the Confederate advance reached Westport days before the battle. Regardless of allegiance, for the farms south of Westport—including those in the Waldo area—the news was cause for worry. Whatever could be done to protect themselves, the homesteaders did it. Provisions were buried or hidden in cellars and barns. Livestock was moved, if there was a chance to get the animals out of the path of the oncoming armies. And of course, any available ammunition was stockpiled and secured.

By this time, Price's army consisted of 8,500 men, of the 22,000 soldiers with which he had started the raid into Missouri. But his supply train had grown. He traveled with more than five hundred wagons and more than five thousand livestock. Now all that—soldiers, livestock and wagons—would have to ford the Blue River to reach Westport. The selected spot was Byram's Ford, near present-day Swope Park on Sixty-third Street. They were on their third consecutive day of fighting. The Union was there to meet them, but the Confederates prevailed and moved their fighting forces across the Blue River. To take the wagons across the Blue would take too much time and effort. The decision was made to send the wagons southward, away from the fighting, to reconnoiter at New Santa Fe.

On the other side of the Blue, the Confederate troops moved southwest, along Town Fork Creek, to where South Broadland Church sits today near Seventy-ninth Street and Holmes Road. This was the farm of the Mockbee family, another of the area's large landholders. There, the two sides met in what Paul Kirkman describes in his book *The Battle of Westport* as "some of the most intense fighting of the day." The fighting pitted the Rebel cavalry against a group from the Kansas Militia, armed with a twenty-four-pound howitzer cannon. When the rebels grew tired of the cannon blowing holes into their ranks, they mounted a full-on cavalry charge accompanied by the famed "rebel yell." The tactic worked. The assault claimed one hundred souls on the Union side, with just as many prisoners and untold wounded. The cannon bursts, the thundering of the horses and the piercing rebel yell could be heard for miles around, sending civilians within earshot into hiding.

Farther north, nearer to Westport, face-offs and maneuverings between the two sides set the stage for the big fight. The Battle of Westport is sometimes called the "Gettysburg of the West," comparing the Confederacy's similar objectives of invading enemy territory, and that following both engagements, the Confederacy's advance was permanently stopped. But Westport was neither as costly nor as long a battle as Gettysburg. From the standpoint of those in the path of the Battle of Westport, the dwellers on the farms south of Westport, this is a distinction without difference.

The battle started early on a frosty Sunday morning on October 23, 1864. The Confederate soldiers were positioned on the south banks of

Brush Creek, roughly the current site of Loose Park near Fifty-first Street and Wornall Road. The Union forces fought from the creek's north side and held the area between the creek and Westport. The Confederacy had strategic control of everything south of the creek, including the farm and home of John Wornall, which they quickly commandeered for a hospital.

Wornall was another of the city's prominent landholders and businessmen. His homestead, near what is now Sixty-first Street and Wornall Road, was a local landmark, and the road that ran south from Westport to connect with the trails already was known as "Wornall Lane." As a property owner in this part of the county, Wornall was on a par with David Waldo. Late in her life, John Wornall's third wife, Roma, recalled the days just before the battle, saying, "The beautiful Indian Summer days had come. Nature was glorious in the glowing colors of the crimson, brown and yellow leaves. The dwellers of the busy little city of Kansas were pursuing their peaceful occupations and business was brisk when a disturbing alarm was heard. News items of Price's Raid were eagerly read. A long week of fearful days, of wild rumors passed by."

Despite the fact that Wornall was a slaveholder, the Wornall homestead was afforded no particular respect by the troops. They were in the midst of a battle—a battle they were quickly losing—and so only a modicum of respect was paid to the family, and none to the property, for the accommodation. When the South evacuated the house and started its retreat down Wornall Lane, the Wornall house was commandeered again by the Union army, again in service as a hospital. The Union army was no more courteous than the Confederates had been. The Wornall House history records that once the fighting had finally left the Wornall property, there were mounds of amputated limbs in the yard, naked of any sign of which side their former owners had served.

The fleeing Confederate army continued south, taking up positions as it could to try to mount another attack and reverse the momentum. They made a final defense along today's Gregory Boulevard (Seventy-first Street), in a flank that ran at least from the state line east to what is now Troost Avenue, using stone walls of farms as their barricades. The effort was to no avail. South of Gregory Boulevard, the Confederacy was in full retreat, and the Union was in hot pursuit.

It was not a swift exodus for either side, dragging the heavy artillery, bearing the wounded and dead on wagons and stretchers. The long columns of men and machinery took hours to move south through the area. The Confederacy, in its retreat, scavenged what they could from every available farm. The Union, relentless in its chase of the vanquished, scoured every house and outbuilding for signs of renegades or ambushers. No wonder that for a time "Wornall Lane" came to be known as "Bloody Lane."

The battle consumed the entire day. For the soldiers moving south, there would be more fighting. But in the farms south of Westport, there was only the relief of the battle's conclusion and the horror of what it left in its wake. The countryside was littered with broken wagons, dead horses, dead and dying men. More houses than the Wornalls' became hospitals that day and for days afterward, as the Union began to regroup and repair itself. And while women in the area took to nursing the wounded regardless of their uniform, men turned their farms into cemeteries, as the dead of all species were hastily buried before contagion set in.

It would have been hard for those who lived through that day to imagine a time when their lives would return to normal or a day when their fortunes would turn from despair to hope. They could not know that, even as war raged, there were those in Kansas City who had already laid plans for prosperity.

The Economic Steam Engine—Waldo and the Railroads

Kansas City's existence was rooted in the network of wagon trails that had moved the nation westward, but the wagons did not secure its permanence. Steam locomotion would do that. The railroads would be Kansas City's ticket to the future. And Waldo would come along for the ride.

Even before the Civil War, Kansas City's most prominent and influential citizens were planning for the bigger role they wanted the city to play in the nation's economy. Their ambitions had far outgrown what was still a comparatively small town by eastern standards, and a rough and muddy one at that. The railroads had been stretching west for years. As early as the 1830s, political interests in Missouri were starting to charter railroads, albeit ones that were never built. Too many events conspired to keep progress from moving forward very rapidly—economic downturns and the Civil War among them. While the railroads were being widely used around the country, few were visionary enough to see their full potential. Rail was still largely seen as a means of connecting one place directly with another.

The idea of a network of railroads, let alone something as ambitious as a rail that spanned the continent, seemed unrealistic.

But as times improved and the vision of a rail system began to emerge, Missouri was well positioned to take advantage. True, when President Lincoln finally approved a line to the West Coast that ran through Omaha, Kansas City missed its first chance. But the locals believed that many other opportunities were coming their way. Two railroads in particular offered promise. The Pacific Railroad was laying track out of St. Louis on the south side of the Missouri River, and the Hannibal and St. Joseph Railroad was moving forward on the north. But therein was the dilemma for Kansas City. No railroad had yet bridged the Missouri River, and neither seemed inclined to do so. While the city itself was on the south side of the river, the Pacific Railroad's line would not run that far north when it reached Missouri's western edge. The Hannibal and St. Joseph's line would run too far north, and on the other side of the river. It would be up to the vested interests in Kansas City to find a way to connect their city to a railroad. The way, they decided, was a bridge. Now all that was left was to convince a railroad that building a bridge would make money. It was a monumental task.

Trade was on Kansas City's side. The trails had long established the area as a major route for livestock as well as goods from Mexico. How much better it would be for the country's markets to have ready access to those goods by rail—and how much better for Kansas City, too. But making that happen was still an uphill climb. A bridge and all that would come with it would require capital and the support of every Kansas City business the local leadership could muster. Beyond that, a deal would have to be struck with a railroad. Every community in the state was clamoring to connect to a railroad.

The competition was narrowed to Kansas City and Leavenworth, Kansas. Before the war, Kansas City wasn't even given serious consideration. Leavenworth, with more than seven thousand residents, was almost twice the size of Kansas City. Largely due to its military fort, Leavenworth was well-known back east, while Kansas City was virtually unknown. After the war, the comparison was even less favorable. Leavenworth's population was now nearly four times that of Kansas City, and Kansas City had earned a broad reputation as filthy, backward and still sympathetic to the South. It took a great deal of civic aggrandizement and the assistance of former newspaperman, mayor and now U.S. Congressman Robert Van Horn to pull it all off. But in the end, Kansas City won. The Hannibal and St. Joseph Railroad would build a bridge across the Missouri River, leading straight south into the heart of downtown Kansas City.

It came to be known as the Hannibal Bridge or, more simply, "the Bridge." It opened in 1869, and as predicted, Kansas City's fortunes immediately turned upward. Even before the bridge opened, speculators snatched up property that would forever determine the character of the Kansas City landscape. The bottomland next to the river, just west of the city's bluffs, became highly valuable for its proximity to the bridge. The fact that a river bottom would be prone to flooding seemed of little concern, weighed against the speculative value of the location. Ironworks and lumber mills sprouted up in support of the bridge's construction, creating Kansas City's first industrial sector. In 1870, the year after the bridge opened, Kansas City's population jumped to an astounding thirty-two thousand, about eight times its size only five years before. Leavenworth, with just eighteen thousand residents, was left in the dust. Of course, the result of all this growth was urban chaos. Kansas City sprawled out, and as it did, it took the bedlam, the muck and the tribulations of a growing city with it. Much of the city's growth was south, in the area between downtown and Westport, which was then still an independent city.

Once again, a man of vision saw an answer, and the answer again was rail, of a sort. As a native New Yorker, Nehemiah Holmes was familiar with horse-drawn railcars. They had run in New York City since the 1830s. Holmes had come to Kansas City before the Civil War and found success working in insurance and finance. Before that, he had run a store. Nothing in his background suggested to anyone with capital or influence that Holmes knew anything about transportation. But he was smart and persuasive. Holmes understood which route would best serve the expanding city. Five months before the Hannibal Bridge was officially opened, Holmes incorporated a business he called the Kansas City and Westport Horse Rail Road Company. Because the cars ran on rails laid into the streets, Holmes also had to forge an agreement with the city for use of the streets. There were restrictions, rate caps and a responsibility for maintaining the streets he used, but in exchange, the City of Kansas City granted Holmes an exclusive twenty-year franchise on the route. Less than two years after the company had been formed, Nehemiah Holmes opened the route to operation. He began serving the downtown area, but it would be almost another two years used to accumulate revenue before service was extended to the promised southern terminus at Westport.

One of the cars of Nehemiah Holmes's early Kansas City and Westport Horse Rail Road Company. *Missouri Valley Special Collections, Kansas City Public Library, Kansas City, MO.*

The line itself was not a great moneymaker, but it served the changing needs of a growing population, who now lived too distant from their places of work to walk. Similar services appeared elsewhere, reaching to growing areas east and west of downtown. For the next twenty years, off and on as the economy rose or fell, the lines continued to shift and ultimately grow into an interurban system of connections that allowed people from Kansas City to travel all the way to Westport in the course of a day. Eventually, the horse-drawn rail cars were replaced by more modern cable-driven railways, which in turn were replaced with cars driven by that marvel of the late-nineteenth century, electricity. With all these improvements, the ride itself was made only slightly more pleasant. It was a trip made at a snail's pace over rough rails in uncomfortable cars. But it beat walking.

Meanwhile, far to the south, the Missouri Pacific Railroad (formerly the Pacific) had finally reached the western edge of Missouri. Its aim was to extend southwest to serve the agricultural markets there. The Missouri Pacific line was a long way from Kansas City's Hannibal Bridge and the only rail service that the city enjoyed. But a connection of about eight miles north to Westport—that was possible. A site was chosen near where the tracks ran close to the Blue River. The place became known as Dodson, named for a local landowner. The connecting railroad was incorporated as the Kansas City and Westport Belt Railway Company, tying it by the name to Nehemiah Holmes's earlier enterprise. Ultimately it would become known mostly as the Dodson "dummy" line. "Dummy" referred to the practice of making the small steam locomotives look like anything but what they were. The engines were noisy and smelly. They frightened horses and irritated those who had to live by the tracks. So the engines were muffled and dressed up to look more like streetcars than trains, hence the name "dummy." The Dodson line was perfectly suited as a dummy line. The population so far south was still pretty thin.

In the spring of 1894, the owners of the railroad, now called the Kansas City Electric Railway, changed the name to the Westport and Waldo Railroad. An 1894 article in the *Westport Sentinel Examiner* explained the change:

> *The old name did not locate the road. Kansas City is the best and most taken name on the American continent, and it should not be taken in vain and applied in such a way as to be misleading. Westport may not be quite as well known as Kansas City but when the home seeker reaches the latter place every good real estate agent will at once advise him to locate his wife and children in Westport, where there is an abundance of pure air and southern breezes.*

Understandably, the *Westport Sentinel Examiner* was in the business of promoting Westport. But that didn't matter to those at the other end of the

A 1930s-era streetcar headed south out of the Waldo Station near Seventy-fourth Street and Broadway Avenue. *Wilborn & Associates.*

This 1894 advertisement in the *Westport Sentinel Examiner* for David Waldo Jr.'s Waldo Land & Investment Company shows the short-lived Waldo Horse Race Track. *Missouri Valley Special Collections, Kansas City Public Library, Kansas City, MO.*

line. It was the Westport and Waldo Railroad. Waldo had a railroad. Waldo was officially on the map.

The engines were more than tolerated in Waldo. They were welcomed. Every farmer and craftsman in the area now had the option to put his goods on the Dodson line and send it up to Westport. More land speculation came to Waldo. Large parcels were split and acres purchased, hoping to capitalize on the proximity to the rail. The tracks ran just east of John Wornall's house. They passed lumberyards and feedlots and orchards. The Dodson line was largely commercial, but a couple of times a day, a passenger car would be attached. To take advantage of that traffic, David Waldo Jr., now in control of his father's property, built and promoted a horseracing track for a while in the early 1890s, but it soon closed.

Now the people, as well as the goods, of Waldo could easily get to Westport and even to downtown. As Waldo approached the turn of the century, the folks who lived there were excited about their prospects. They were riding the rails into a horizon they could not yet clearly see, but that could only be better than the bloody past still fresh in their memories.

Waldo's Earliest and Most Enduring Enterprises

With the advent of the railroad, Waldo was primed for growth. The businesses that were already there in the late 1800s were farms and ranches and a few businesses that supported them. Those that were there had already started to cluster around present-day Seventy-fifth Street and Wornall Road. But this was still a rural place. Kansas City's boundaries only reached to Forty-ninth Street by 1897. Another twelve years would pass before the city limit reached any part of Waldo.

One of the earliest structures, and one of the last to fall, was a livery stable on the southwest corner of Seventy-fifth Street and Wornall Road. It was a low, inconsequential building made largely of stone. Because that corner was originally part of the Alexander Majors property, speculation has been that the livery belonged to the Majors descendants. However, at the turn of the century, a doctor named Gosling had a house on that corner, and the building could have belonged to him. In the modern era, the building became known as "the Rock Barn." For years, it was

The "rock barn" near Seventy-fifth Street and Wornall Road—believed to be one of the first structures in Waldo—before it was demolished in 1997. *Betty Tillotson.*

part of the operations of Jasper's, a renowned Waldo area restaurant. Jasper's companion eatery, the more casual Marco Polo Trattoria, used the barn for storage. The property was sold in 1997 to make way for a new drugstore. The rock barn was demolished shortly thereafter, with no fanfare. Insufficient documentation on the building's origins or significance prevented it from gaining historical protection.

In 1907, a young Waldo resident named William O'Keefe had just returned to town following a visit to the St. Louis World's Fair. There, he had seen his first panoramic picture and was keen to try it himself. He asked Dr. Gosling if he could come in his house and take pictures from the upstairs window, which faced north. The pictures he pasted together created the first photographic account of life in Waldo. On the east side of Wornall Road, nearest Seventy-fifth Street, Croner's Store is shown in its first Waldo location. The store faced the railroad tracks and was within a few feet of a newly built powerhouse for the newly electrified railroad. Looking north to the horizon, the fields are still farmland, but the first electric power poles already line the corner. The railroad had brought electrification to Waldo.

On the northwest corner of Seventy-fifth Street and Wornall Road, O'Keefe's camera caught the signs of excavation and foundation work that

This section of William O'Keefe's 1907 panoramic photo of Waldo looking north on Wornall from Seventy-fifth Street shows the Broadway M.E. Church in its original location at Stewart's livery. *Betty Tillotson.*

Pitkin Hall at Seventy-fifth Street and Wornall Road, as it appeared in 1940, was one of the first commercial structures built in Waldo, erected in 1907. *Kansas City (MO) Landmarks Commission.*

would soon be Pitkin Hall. The red brick building was built in a simple, functional style, a significant investment for its time and place. By 1919, Pitkin Hall was home to South Side Savings and Loan, Waldo's first bank. At one time, there were apartments on the second floor. Just west of the Pitkin Hall building site stood the home and blacksmith shop of a man named Stewart. The Broadway Methodist Church was born in that blacksmith shop. Neighbors paid a small admission fee to come in and listen to a gramophone play a recording of the popular opera star Enrico Caruso. The proceeds

Waldo Grain Company—shown here circa 1920—is Waldo's longest continually operating business. *Waldo Area Business Association.*

were used to start the church's building fund. Until that sanctuary could be built, the newly formed congregation met upstairs in Pitkin Hall. While the blacksmith shop is long gone, Pitkin Hall remains. Ice damage in the winter of 2007 caused significant damage to Pitkin Hall's roof and façade, with the fortunate outcome that the masonry work and windows were restored, ensuring that Pitkin Hall will remain a Waldo landmark and business center for generations to come.

Beyond the view of William O'Keefe's panoramic photograph, other businesses were starting to populate Waldo. The Waldo Grain Company was just around the corner to the south from Dr. Gosling's property, at 7512 Wornall Road. Started in 1916, it is today Waldo's longest continually operating business and remains owned by members of the Frey family, the original owners. Waldo Grain found its first market selling feed to the area farmers, but when it relocated to its present site at 7801 Wornall Road about ten years later, they were also selling grass seed and gardening supplies to all the new households springing up around Waldo. As another generation passed, pet food was added.

Spangler's Stop & Shop Market on Seventy-fifth Street, as it appeared in the 1930s, was one of many area Waldo grocers. *Betty Tillotson and Norma Spangler Virden.*

Many different businesses have endured long enough to become a part of Waldo's history for the simple fact of their impressive staying power. A few of these mainstays of Waldo are listed here. Because Waldo was annexed into the city in phases spanning a number of years, records of business locations and tenure are not complete. This list has been gleaned from available business listings, maps, photographs and personal anecdotes.

Each business is listed (with name changes in parentheses) with its original address and the approximate period it was located in Waldo (although not always in the same location). Some records list addresses that today are considered Wornall Road addresses, but during Waldo's early period, the street names "Broadway" and "Wornall Road" were sometimes used interchangeably. In addition, prior to 1930, Gregory Boulevard was known only as Seventy-first Street. Business locations of that era are listed with the Seventy-first Street address.

30 to 40 Years:

- Crown Drug —7100 Wornall Road, 1925–1955.
- Murphy's Drug Store—Seventy-fifth Street and Wornall Road, 1907–1940.
- Southside Savings & Loan—7423 Wornall Road, 1919–1950.
- Dierk's & Sons Lumber Company—Seventy-fifth Street and Wornall Road, 1919–1955.
- Waldo Recreation (first billiards, later bowling)—512 West Seventy-fifth Street, circa 1925–1960.

40 to 50 Years:

- Land Chevrolet (later Pappas Chevrolet)—119 West Gregory Boulevard, 1935–1980.
- Milen's Dry Goods (later Milen's Department Store)—7416 Wornall Road, 1925–1972.
- Westhaven Hotel—7431 Broadway, 1930–1980.

50 to 60 Years:

- Great Atlantic & Pacific Tea Company (A&P Grocery)—125 West Seventy-fifth Street, 1925–1980.
- Swyden Cleaners—329 East Gregory Boulevard, 1955–present.
- Turley, Dr. John J., Optometrist—200 West Seventy-fifth Street, 1955–present.
- Gunter Pest Management—220 West Seventy-second Street, 1950–present.
- McLain's Bakery—7422 Wornall Road, 1950–present (relocated 2011 to Gregory Boulevard).

60 to 70 Years:

- Betty Tillotson's Studio of Dance—209 East Gregory Blvd., 1950–present.
- Katz Drug Company (later Skaggs, Osco and CVS)—333 West Seventy-fifth Street, 1945–present.
- Romanelli Grill—7122 Wornall Road, 1940–2005.
- Little Red Hen Poultry (later Hen House Grocery)—8230 Wornall Road, 1940–present.

75 Years or More:

- Evans Lime Company (later Evans Trent)—Seventy-ninth Terrace and Wornall Road, 1924–2000.
- Waldo Grain—7801 Wornall Road, 1916–present.

Chapter 3

1900–1940: DRESSED IN OVERALLS

Opportunity is missed by most people because it is dressed in overalls and looks like work.
—Thomas Edison

Location, timing and a bit of luck were enough to get Waldo started, but not enough to make it grow. For that, it would take hard work, dedication and even love. After nearly sixty years of life, there was now a second and third generation of people who loved Waldo and called it home. They were dedicated to seeing it grow. As the nineteenth century became the twentieth, Waldo would need that dedication. The railroad and the trails were opportunities claimed by Waldo's first generations. Waldo's next generation would face a lot of trials before finding an opportunity of its own.

For the first few years of the twentieth century, folks in Waldo had plenty of reason to wonder what that next great opportunity might be. Stagnant growth was the result of a great national paranoia that stemmed from an unstable economy, the First World War and history's greatest pandemic. The latter hit Kansas City especially hard. In the last six months of 1918, more than two thousand people died of the so-called Spanish Influenza, making Kansas City one of the most stricken cities in the nation. City health officials took drastic measures to curb its spread. Schools, churches, motion picture houses—any place, public or private, where people gathered was ordered to limit its customers to no more than twenty at a time. Hotels, restaurants, cabarets and even the streetcar lines suffered from lack of business.

The Spanish flu epidemic was only the latest catastrophe to strike the city. In the first two decades of the new century, Kansas City had been beset by several major floods in the west bottoms, fires that separately decimated the brand-new convention center and the stockyards and a streetcar workers strike so contentious that it prompted the National Guard's assistance after some of the cars were dynamited.

Notwithstanding, Waldo had seen a bit of growth during these years. When the rails in Waldo were electrified in 1907, it brought electricity to Waldo. A few brave souls built buildings and started businesses near the powerhouse at of Seventy-fifth Street and Wornall Road. They were small businesses, the type that might be anyplace. But grocers, banks and churches are the stuff that make a community. Thinking—or hoping—more people were coming that way, the old farmsteads were regularly put up for sale, once again in the spirit of speculation that was becoming Waldo's trademark. This far south of the city, however, residential development was fitful. In the 1890s, David Waldo Jr. had taken some of his father's property and offered it up for new housing. He'd even built a racetrack on part of the property near Holmes Road. He banked on the notion that folks in Kansas City might enjoy a place to come out into the country, watch the ponies run and thrill at the prospect of a winning bet. But the Waldo Race Track never really got off the ground and closed after just a couple of years. Others were trying it too, with middling success. And a few others, particularly brave souls, built large homes along Wornall, supposedly imagining that they, too, would one day be in the midst of the Country Club District.

When, in 1909, Kansas City extended its southern boundary from Forty-ninth Street to Seventy-seventh Street, Waldo—or at least a part of Waldo—officially became part of Kansas City. The annexation was due in no small part to J.C. Nichols. Nichols was more than just one of the several developers who was speculating on the city's growth. Through the work of the Nichols Company, he had been quietly and methodically building homes. The way he was doing it would revolutionize the national housing industries for generations to come. Nichols was working on a grand plan he marketed as the "Country Club District." He started in 1905 just south of Brush Creek with a housing subdivision originally called Bismark Place. For the next decade, Nichols purchased, optioned or developed acre after acre of the farmsteads south of the creek. In 1919, he opened his first commercial development near the old Border Star School at Sixty-third Street and Wornall Road, calling it the Brookside Shops after the creek that followed the Dodson dummy line tracks that rambled through the center of the district. Nichols designed the Brookside Shops to provide all the necessities for the new houses, which were decidedly upscale. This was a good sign for Waldo. Folks there could literally see prosperity coming their way. Here, at last, was the opportunity for the Waldo's current generation. Waldo dressed itself in overalls and went to work.

Waldo became a construction hub. Building all those fine homes that the Nichols Company and other developers were planning would require materials—and lots of them. The great burst of enterprise that took place in the 1920s and forever formed the character of Waldo focused on that most basic of industries, building materials. Once again, location was in Waldo's favor. They were just on the southern edge of Kansas City's great housing boom of the '20s, and they had a rail line that could bring raw materials straight up from the Missouri Pacific railhead at Dodson to a company's loading dock.

One of the first such businesses to set up shop in Waldo was Dierk's & Sons Lumber Company, a well-known area lumber dealer. The Waldo location was the company's latest. Their office and lumberyard nestled right against the railroad tracks on the south side of Seventy-fifth Street. Through the 1920s, the ranks of these companies swelled to include cement plants, metal shops, building contractors, nurseries and greenhouses. There were woodlots and coal companies to supply the fuel for industrial furnaces. The local blacksmith now offered welding services to keep Waldo's industrial machinery working. The demand for ice was so great that Waldo could support two ice plants, one on Gregory Boulevard and another just four blocks south on Seventy-fifth Street.

Having two ice plants in Waldo was a real milestone. They were run by competing firms, the Western Ice Service Company, which operated at 201 West Gregory Boulevard, and the City Ice Company of Kansas City, operating on Seventy-fifth Street just east of Broadway. The City Ice Company published a monthly magazine in the 1920s, the *City Ice Man*. The magazine promoted the company, of course, and sprinkled its pages with homilies on the benefits of refrigeration. They also included features of community interest. In 1925, an article entitled "Waldo, A Beautiful City of Homes," featured a pictorial layout of Waldo's commercial and community landmarks and a few of the area's large new homes belonging to notable bankers, doctors and business leaders.

The singular exception to this forming character of Waldo stood at its northern edge. The Nichols Company, anticipating housing projects

Dierk's & Sons Lumber Company, one of Waldo's earliest businesses, located its office on Seventy-fifth Street directly east of the railroad tracks for ease of delivery. *Kansas City (MO) Landmarks Commission.*

Trucks await delivery at the Waldo plant of City Ice Company of Kansas City, circa 1932. *Missouri Valley Special Collections, Kansas City Public Library, Kansas City, MO.*

This photo montage in a 1925 edition of *City Ice Man* accompanied an article extolling the "new" community of Waldo. *Missouri Valley Special Collections, Kansas City Public Library, Kansas City, MO.*

they had in the adjacent acreage, built the Romanelli Shops at Gregory Boulevard and Wornall Road in 1922. Just as with Brookside, the Romanelli Shops reflected Nichols's belief that commercial buildings should blend stylistically with the houses around it. While the Brookside Shops show English Tudor influences, the Romanelli Shops construction reflects more of a Beaux Arts styling, with its mansard roof, rusticated stonework corners and decorative garlands. Such high style was used as a sign to potential residents that this was an affluent community. The Nichols Company developed other commercial centers along Gregory all the way east to Oak Street, forever creating a different sort of commercial character on Gregory than existed elsewhere in Waldo. But in Waldo, Gregory was as far south as the Nichols Company's commercial interests ever ventured.

By the 1930s, the building frenzy had slowed, in large part to the Great Depression. By now, though, the nature of business in Waldo

Cars line up along the newly opened Romanelli Shops at Gregory Boulevard and Wornall Road, 1931. *Wilborn & Associates.*

shifted from building to maintaining all these new homes. In time, Waldo would have its share of dress shops and dime stores, but once again in times of trial, Waldo found its niche serving the more prosaic needs of the Country Club District's households, who, feeling the pinch of the Depression too, were spending more on necessities than luxuries. Even though the Depression caused many a business to close, there always seemed to be another one opening. Hardware stores, plumbing repair shops, electricians and furniture stores became a permanent fixture of the Waldo business landscape.

By now, Waldo stretched much farther south than the intersection of Seventy-fifth Street and Wornall Road. But the city limits stopped at Seventy-seventh Street in Waldo. The rest of Waldo would not be annexed until after World War II. Waldo's place on the fringe of Kansas City civilization had made it a somewhat ragged, irregular community, part fashionable residential, part scruffy industrial. But as housing development crept ever closer and the war years put a temporary stop on investment, which of Waldo's two emerging faces would dominate remained anyone's guess.

The Community Builders—J.C. Nichols and Napoleon Dible

Those that had bet on rail had bet wisely. Kansas City was catapulted into the national economic arena. Every day carried a new breed of fortune hunter to Kansas City. The town was used to the traffic, but it was more accustomed to serving their needs and then sending them on their way. This group intended to stay, lured by the jobs created by those railroads, the stockyards and all the other new industry. Now came the question—where would they live?

In fact, Kansas City's population boom was happening in many of the newer cities in the country, particularly west of the Mississippi. There were subtle changes in the wind that would, over the next half century, draw more and more people away from the farms and into the cities in search of the opportunities only a big city could provide. But the fact that Kansas City wasn't unique was no comfort in dealing with such tremendous growth. It was almost beyond the city's ability to keep up with traffic, sanitation, crime and housing. In 1900, Kansas City's population was slightly more than 150,000 people, already a huge increase over the pre-railroad boom that brought the total to 32,000. Ten years later, it reached 250,000. By 1930, it had sailed past the 350,000 mark.

Kansas City and the nation were in the throes of a housing boom, fueled on the development side by ready access to capital and land and on the homebuyer's side by immigration, industrial wages that provided a higher standard of living and, most particularly, the automobile. With the automobile, a person had options where to work, where to shop and where to live. In Kansas City, the increasingly popular choice for all those was to the south. Even with the opening of a second bridge spanning the Missouri River in 1910—one that gave access not just to trains but to cars and pedestrians too and that opened up real estate for development so convenient to downtown—the predominant growth was to the south.

The housing boom would prove the source of fortune for the next generation of Kansas City leaders, just as the trails and the rails had done for their fathers and grandfathers. Few would enjoy the success and long careers of the gentlemen most influential in the building of Waldo's neighborhoods—J.C. Nichols and N.W. Dible.

Jesse Clyde Nichols came to the development profession early. Other than his early years trucking produce in from the grange his father ran in Olathe,

Increased development along Seventy-fifth Street just east of Wornall Road shows how much the city had extended south by the 1930s. *Wilborn & Associates.*

Kansas, and a flirtation with a legal career during his college days, land development was the only endeavor he ever pursued. He was taken with a question posed to him by a real estate professor in law school. Why didn't Americans treat their homes as legacy investments as the Europeans did? He saw the answer around him in Kansas City at the turn of the century. Squalor and pestilence, crowding and poor infrastructure and the seeming luxury of unlimited land only encouraged people to continually relocate. He saw, too, that in their exodus, they only added to the blighted conditions they were trying to escape.

In 1905, Nichols took the first step in what was to be his life's work—the development of the Country Club District. Starting with just a few parcels below Brush Creek, just south of Westport, he started by building houses. But even then, his sights were set on something far greater than a few homes. Nichols was quiet and hardworking, the sort who appeared unassuming on first meeting. But he had an unshakeable belief in his vision. That conviction emboldened him as he successively met and won over many of the city's most important businessmen. They gave him something he needed to make his vision work. Capital could be gathered from many sources, but to change the face of the city as he planned, he needed their endorsement. He needed them to help him through city hall, to trust him to develop their property, to demonstrate their confidence by buying his most impressive homes. For the most part, Nichols had that endorsement through his entire career. By the time he died in 1950 at the age of sixty-nine, Nichols was not only Kansas City's most famous real estate developer, he was also the embodiment of the professional standard within the industry. His national influence on housing and commercial development was profound and remains so to this day. His ideas were revolutionary at the start of his career—incorporating commercial development within the neighborhoods, creating activities and amenities within the residential areas and using neighborhood associations to strengthen and bind residents to their communities—but at his death, they were accepted practices.

These ideas were predicated on a real philosophy Nichols had about development. He believed that property values could be stabilized by first encouraging the wealthiest of residents to locate and, most importantly, to stay invested in their new neighborhood. From there, stability would breed more stability and neighborhoods could be added to serve a wider range of incomes. To secure that loyalty, Nichols would do what it took to give them value they wouldn't find elsewhere. There would be shops nearby, handpicked from among the city's finest merchants. There would be plenty of parks and winding, tree-lined streets that would be a joy to drive down in their new automobiles. Nichols made sure there were schools and churches nearby. He invited activities like community field days and neighborhood garden shows to bring neighbors and neighborhoods together. He published a monthly newsletter that gave lots of tips about maintaining a new home.

Kansas Citians responded in throngs. With regular progress, the Nichols Company developments continued south from Brush Creek for fifteen years, until in 1919 they reached the unassuming intersection of Sixty-third Street and Wornall Road. There, Nichols built his first commercial development, the Brookside Shops. The shops offered everything the newly affluent, newly relocated Country Club District resident could need or simply want. From meat markets to dance schools, from hardware stores to the latest in women's fashions, the Brookside Shops had it all. And all of it was within sight of Waldo. A few years later, when the Nichols Company started commercial development along

Gregory Boulevard with the Romanelli Shops at Wornall Road, Nichols's development wasn't just within sight, it was within reach.

The Nichols Company was largely responsible for the neighborhoods along Waldo's northern boundary. One of the largest is Armour Hills, situated north of Gregory Boulevard between Wornall Road and Oak Street. The neighborhood is named for the meatpacking family dynasty from whom Nichols had purchased the acreage. The development was announced in 1922, and the Armour Hills Homes Association agreement and deed restrictions were among the first of many the Nichols Company filed that year. The type of housing in Armour Hills was still high quality, but it was smaller in scale than Nichols's earlier developments. The market Nichols was targeting was no longer just the elite. There were plenty of middle-income families that needed housing too, and it was part of Nichols's vision to serve households all along the economic spectrum.

This aerial photo shows the new construction of the Nichols Company's Armour Hills development in 1925, while the property to the west (bottom) is open fields. *Wilborn & Associates.*

Just five years later in 1930, both the Armour Hills (top) and Romanelli Gardens (bottom) subdivisions were essentially complete. *Missouri Valley Special Collections, Kansas City Public Library, Kansas City, MO.*

The following year, the first plat of the Armour Fields neighborhood was filed, a neighborhood just east of Wornall Road across from Armour Hills. Next came Romanelli Gardens, at the northwest corner of Gregory Boulevard and Wornall Road. During the early 1920s, these and other Nichols developments were continually being expanded with new plats and tinkered with in style and amenities. Armour Hills, for example, had its own golf course for a short time. Another example is a commercial development that Nichols initially planned at Brookside Road and Sixty-ninth Street, just east of the streetcar line. A special streetcar stop was built, and access across Wornall Road was provided beneath the track's elevated line. The district was to be called "Armour Center," but in the end, he decided the nearby Romanelli Shops had rendered it unnecessary, and so the parcels that had originally been planned for commercial development were converted to housing.

These developments were the closest the Nichols Company would come to direct involvement in Waldo's growth. In 1925, the housing boom turned

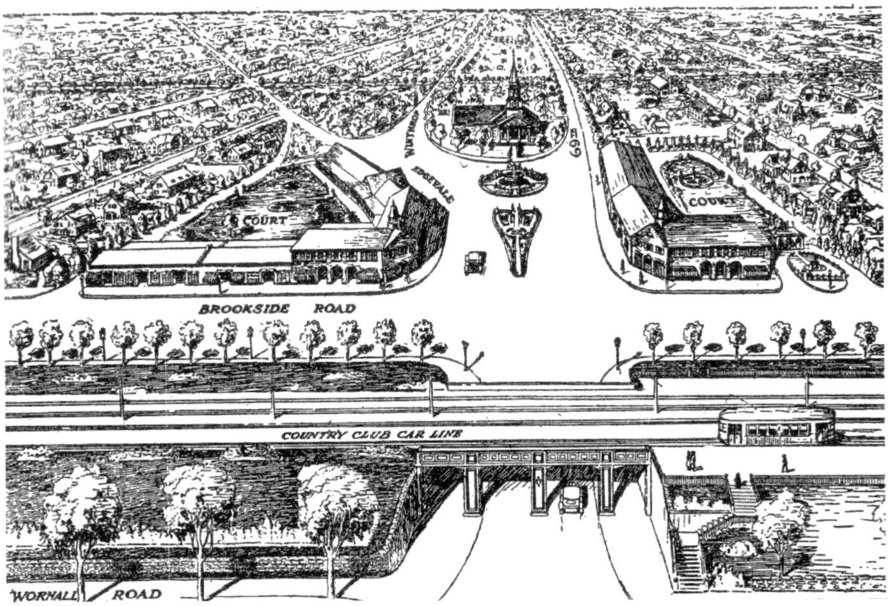

This promotional piece from the Nichols Company shows a planned (but never built) commercial development on Sixty-ninth Street, adjacent to the streetcar line. *Waldo Area Business Association.*

to bust. It had been a record year in Kansas City, with more than 3,600 single residences constructed. By the following year, there were nearly a third fewer. All over the country, developers were facing the consequences of building beyond what the market could bear. Similar to the Kansas City experience, nationally there were more than a million single-home starts in 1925. Five years later, there were half that many, and three years later, at the depths of the Great Depression, only 100,000 homes were started across the entire country.

While Nichols's development slowed during these lean years, it did not stop completely. But those who might have supposed Nichols would continue southward once the good times returned had not been paying attention. From the outset, the Nichols Company had moved south—and west. Some of its most expensive properties were just across the state line in a community it created named Mission Hills. The spine of the Nichols development lay not along Wornall Road, but along State Line, and in the

The Westhaven was brand new in this photo from the 1930s and, as a hotel, a unique addition to the Waldo community. *Dave and Bette Smith.*

years ahead, the Kansas side of the metro would see most of the Nichols Company's investment.

Ironically, Waldo's existing development was likely one reason for Nichols's lack of interest in moving farther south. The heart of Waldo was already built up, and even then, developers preferred so-called "green field" development. It was easier to dig holes in unbroken ground than work around or condemn existing development. It's also likely that, as much of Waldo lay beyond the city limits, Nichols thought the extra effort required to annex and then impose the necessary land use regulations wasn't worth the reward. He had gone through that tedious work when he had the city boundary moved to Seventy-seventh Street.

Then there was the railroad. The streetcar line had been a blessing and a curse for Nichols from his first housing projects south of Brush Creek. He had claimed it as an amenity back in 1905 when he built the Colonial Shops at Fifty-first and Oak Streets, where the streetcar line became a freight railroad. But he had feared it, too. It was the lifeline for some undesirable businesses—lumberyards and stock pens—that lined the east side of the tracks just south of Brush Creek. He feared it enough to take control of it, in fact. Early on, he organized investors to buy the line and then give it to the Metropolitan Street Railway Company, which was then operating most of the interurban lines in the city. For their part of this generous deal, the "Met," as it was known, was to electrify the route and forever bar freight traffic. They electrified the route, but turned down a $50,000 bonus in favor of keeping the freight option. The quality of the Nichols housing north of Gregory Boulevard had eliminated industrial usage of the rail. South of Gregory, there were now dozens of small operations that all depended on the railroad. In all likelihood, this would have been enough reason for the Nichols Company to focus its future work to the west, rather than south to Waldo.

If the Nichols Company was reticent about developing in and around Waldo, there were plenty of others who were eager to jump in. One of the first was David Milton Proctor, a Waldo resident and respected Kansas City lawyer, former state senator and future city councilman and a muckraker who went on to play an instrumental role in the fall of Boss Tom Pendergast. His home at 7404 Mercier is reported to be the highest point in Kansas City at 301.5 feet above the Missouri River. Proctor formed the Westmoreland Improvement Company, which developed property at the northeast corner of Seventy-fifth Street and Broadway. Proctor's most enduring contribution to Waldo is the Westmoreland Building that sits prominently at that corner. He touted his development as "one hundred acres of the most beautiful ground in Kansas City with a main entrance at Seventy-fourth and Broadway." From his efforts sprang the Waldo-Westmoreland Improvement Association, the first business association in Waldo.

In other areas of Waldo, particularly south of Seventy-fifth Street and east of Wornall Road, housing construction took on a more individualized character. Much of the area was platted right before the housing bust, and as a result, there was no organized development. The houses that were built were scattered, rather than clustered. Many were likely built by those who worked or owned businesses in Waldo, for their personal residences. It would be many years before the area was fully developed.

The dominant developer in Waldo's south side during this period was Napoleon Dible. It was an unlikely name for such a humble man. "N.W.", as he was commonly known, was a contemporary of J.C. Nichols, but unlike Nichols, he came to the development game later in his career. Dible arrived in Kansas City in 1903, a native of Ohio but recently moved from Denver, where he worked in advertising. He made a little money on a minor invention that afforded him the chance to make even more money in railroad stocks. He and his wife came to Kansas City with the thought that Dible would go into business for himself. He sold the railroad stock for start-up capital shortly before the railroad went bankrupt. His banker gave him a lead on a possible venture—another client was a builder looking for a partner. Dible jumped in, seeing the same opportunity that had captivated Nichols and others. The partnership was short-lived. Six months into the venture, the partner skipped town, leaving Dible in the middle of his first project, with no knowledge of housing or construction.

Napoleon W. Dible, one of the most important developers of Waldo area neighborhoods for nearly sixty years. *Missouri Valley Special Collections, Kansas City Public Library, Kansas City, MO.*

Dible was not the type to give up. He was a principled man who took commitments seriously. He was regimented in his personal routine, maintaining a daily schedule that bordered on obsessive. Meals were taken at precisely the same times every day. He neither smoked nor drank and was a devout member of the First Baptist Church and president of its Business Men's Bible Class. In this role, he is credited with having organized the "World's Largest Bible Class," which consisted of more than fifty-two thousand men who met at the city's convention hall in 1923. Despite his faith, he worked tirelessly seven days a week and was never known to take a vacation. He was a lifelong advocate of good health, and at the age of eighty-eight, he wrote a book titled *How to Live One Hundred Years and Retain Your Health and Mental Faculties.*

Dible's disciplined nature, combined with the marketing skills he gathered in advertising, helped him keep the company afloat until he could learn the business. But money was not his principle aim. He was a zealot on the subject of homeownership, determined to provide the middle-class Kansas City family with a home it could afford. To accomplish this, Dible employed

These Dible-built homes demonstrate the developer's most recognizable style—a modified English cottage with dramatic gables and timber-frame details. *Missouri Valley Special Collections, Kansas City Public Library, Kansas City, MO.*

some techniques that were new and innovative. He was among the first to use mass-produced building materials and supplies, buying in bulk and significantly reducing the cost of each home. His floor plans were few and basic, but he managed to find ways to make each home unique inside and out. Architecturally, Dible homes were most typically either a faux English Tudor style—the style most often associated with him—or the arts-and-crafts style of the Prairie School of design often associated with Chicago architects like Frank Lloyd Wright. But Dible also produced a few houses that were innovative for the time, notably the California bungalow form he had once seen in Los Angeles. The style, with its half-second story, provided maximum house on minimally sized lots.

For Nichols, the house was important, but most of his company's deals were about the land development. He built or let others build as opportunity presented. For Dible, the house was what mattered. He built the houses on all his properties and was known to help with financing, moving expenses or whatever it took to get a family into a home. Over the course of his career, N.W. Dible was responsible for the construction of 5,000 homes in thirty-seven subdivisions, a significant number in or near Waldo. On the west side, his largest project was the thousand-unit Ward Park addition that ran from Gregory Boulevard to Seventy-fourth Street, from Wornall Road to the state line. On the east, the Rockhill Gardens and Rockhill Manor subdivisions, from Gregory Boulevard to Eighty-first Street between Oak Street and Troost Avenue, was even larger, with 1,500 homes. When N.W. Dible died in 1960, at the age of eighty-nine, he left the management of the N.W. Dible Company in the hands of his grandsons. He left the community of Waldo with a great legacy of quality neighborhoods that have withstood the test of time.

Merchants of Charity—The Gillis and Armour Homes

Back in those early, heady days of the new railroad, though Kansas City had grown by leaps and bounds, it struggled, too. The needs were great—broken families, unwed mothers, neglected elderly and countless simply toiling through poverty. There were no public agencies to offer assistance, so what little help there was came primarily through the churches. While many in Kansas City were making fortunes, a select group of the fortunate stepped forward to address these struggles. These were the wives of some of Kansas City's wealthiest businessmen.

In 1870, twenty women met to form the Women's Christian Association. Their mission was "to form an organization…to relieve the needy and distressed in this new and struggling city." In short time, their ranks swelled to seventy. The ladies set off in pairs and scoured the city to learn firsthand the nature and extent of the need. They saw the squalor and desperation and were particularly moved by the plight of young women. Through the WCA, they purchased a home at Eleventh and McGee Streets and opened the Working Women's Home to care for "widows [and] young girls in destitute or distressed circumstances." As Christian women, they saw it as their duty to, as they said at the home's opening "to reclaim our erring sisters."

The members of the WCA soon realized, however, that women in distress often came with children in distress. They also were increasingly

The Loose Administrative Building at the Gillis Home campus still serves the organization as it did in this photo taken shortly after it was built in 1929. *The Gillis Center.*

asked to care for foundlings and babies from families that could not afford proper care. So the home was opened to women and children, and when the expanded mission taxed the capacity of their first house, they rented another. The WCA continued to do their best to adapt to the rapid pace of change and growing need. But in 1880, despite their best efforts, the ladies of the WCA could not overcome the long economic depression the country had struggled with for nearly a decade. They were forced to close the program for three years.

Those years were not lost ones. The WCA spent its time in constant fundraising, and in 1883, the program was reopened at yet a third location, this time with outdoor space to accommodate a playground and a garden. Though they continued to face many challenges and near-closures, by 1892, the WCA purchased a second home at Twenty-first Street and Tracy Avenue, where the infants and babies could be separately cared for. Meeting the children's needs so came to dominate their work that the program for women was dropped, and all focus was placed on serving children. But again, that focus was changed when an entirely new opportunity was dropped in the laps of the ladies of the WCA, an opportunity they could scarcely afford to turn down.

Margaret Klock Armour, a member of the WCA and the widow of one of the brothers who founded the Armour Meat Packing Company, offered the group the amazing sum of $25,000 from her husband's estate to establish a home for aged couples, with an additional $5,000 pledge to support a new home for the children. The sum is even more significant when compared to the estimated cost of the entire project, about $33,000. The new facilities were built on land donated by Colonel Thomas Swope. The home for aged couples was christened the Margaret Klock Armour Memorial Home for Aged Couples, but it soon became known as the "Armour Home." The other building was called simply the "Children's Home," but that would soon change, thanks to another WCA member, Mary Gillis Troost. Mrs. Troost was the widow of Dr. Benoist Troost and the niece of William Gillis. The bequest she made to the WCA was intended to honor her uncle and was designated for the maintenance and operation of the children's home. Mrs. Troost stipulated that the home be called the Gillis Home for Children.

Through the 1910s and '20s, the Gillis Home and its sister, the Armour Home, enjoyed widespread support within the Kansas City community and was fairly earning a reputation as an program that made a difference. That reputation was built on the personal involvement of the WCA members in the lives of the "inmates," as was the customary term of the period. This was especially true for the children. The WCA members were each responsible for spending a set number of days working with the children at the home. The ladies never shied from approaching civic organizations, churches and businesses for donations of any kind. The mission of the place and the never-ending need forged their individual commitments to the program and to the maintenance of the facilities. But despite their efforts, by 1924, the buildings were filled to capacity. Just as they were struggling with their next direction, an opportunity presented itself that must have seemed providential.

In 1926, the Western Negro College approached the WCA about buying their campus on Tracy. The $25,000 the college paid allowed the WCA to purchase twenty-six-and-a-half acres "way out in the country" at Eighty-first Street and Wornall Road. The property had been part of the Van Laningham estate and was adjacent to the Sunnyside Dairy. Of the planned move, the *Kansas City Star* reported, "This purchase will cause probably the most beautifully landscaped garden area in Kansas City to be devoted to the playtime hours of the children of the Gillis Orphans' Home and to become the scene of the strolls of those who live

One of the high points each year at the Gillis Home was "Loose Shoe Day," the visit by Mrs. Jacob Loose who brought shoes for all the children. *The Gillis Center.*

at the Armour Memorial Home for Aged Couples." In this corner of Waldo, there was almost no development as yet. The acreage was large, with mature trees and an apple orchard. A lake sat on the property, with a water garden to one side and, on the other, ample room to serve as a swimming hole for the children.

The Gillis Home and the Armour Home would share the property in separate facilities. The architectural firm of Keene and Simpson designed the buildings in the Georgian-style, which gave a stately appearance to the institutions. For the first time, the buildings could be designed with the residents in mind, especially critical when serving the children's needs. Every necessity was considered, including play and study rooms for the children and a small hospital for the elderly. In the end, the total cost for the property and new buildings reached more than $570,000, more than twenty times what the WCA had received for the old property. Most of the gap was filled through the philanthropy of the Loose family, and in tribute, the Loose name was added to the administration building's façade. The campus opened in September 1929.

The physical stability of the homes had been established, but the times were anything but stable. A month after the opening in Waldo, the stock market crashed. Everywhere, there was great need, but no money. In 1934, the Armour Home processed 730 applications, at a time when the average number of residents at the home was eighty-four. It was tough to place children for adoption, but easier by far to place infants, and so during this period, the Gillis Home only served older children. Nationally, social welfare movements increasingly called attention to health and rights issues of the populations the WCA served. Federal and state programs were started where there had been little to none before, and with them came oversight and regulation. The Gillis and Armour Homes always performed at the highest level, but the new rules added costs.

These challenges continued through the 1930s. World War II added more pressures. The Gillis Home and many others like it across the country took in foreign refugee children. Now, even fewer resources were available, gobbled up as they were by the war effort. Institutional rations were even more scrutinized than household rations. In fact, the whole notion of institutional care was called into question. The practice of caring for children was evolving. Institutions seemed cold and impersonal. Alternative programs were being tried and favored.

Yet one boy's story tells of solace found during this time. When a boy named Arsenio came to America in 1942 at the age of ten, he was a refugee who had already spent the first half of his life living in European orphanages. Twenty children traveled with him on a ship that came to New York from war-torn Spain. Only three were put on a train to Kansas City and the Gillis Home. Arsenio spoke no English, but it didn't matter. He assimilated quickly and relatively easily. The letter he wrote to the Gillis Home fifty years later shares nothing but fond memories of the two years he spent there. Like any child who grew up in Waldo, Arsenio recalled walking to school along the streetcar line, arms across shoulders with friends. He wrote of making carts out of roller skates and the sound the wheels made on the concrete. He recalled climbing out the gable window to sit on the roof of the boys' dormitory in the middle of the night, and how the boys all scratched their names in the slate shingles where they sat. He wrote with tenderness of the "two Jewish ladies dressed from head to toe in black" that would take him and the other two refugee children to a park or a restaurant, or to the

In 1942, the Gillis children were entertained by "Peter Pan," mascot for Derby's Peter Pan Peanut Butter, who provided each of the children with their own coloring book. *The Gillis Center.*

airport to watch the planes take off. The ladies didn't speak Spanish, yet despite the lack of conversation, Arsenio felt close to them. He wrote of the kinship he felt with his friends at Gillis, in particular of a boy he had known as "Curley." He wrote only briefly, but unhappily, of his few unsuccessful forays into foster care.

Arsenio's letter to the Gillis Home doesn't detail his life after he left Gillis in 1944, though the letter itself leaves no doubt that he was indelibly changed by his time at Gillis. He closed the letter with his memory of leaving with the social worker who was escorting him to his new home in New York state.

> *The social worker was beaming, she was certain that I would like the new foster home. She knew it was perfect for me. But how could she know? How could she know that living in groups of children since 1936 had become the norm for me, and in what was always an energized environment, that I thrived. She did not know, she could not know, would never know. Her training had taught her to embrace a myth—the family unit is always best.*

After the war, the relationship between the Gillis and Armour Homes and the Waldo community began to flourish. By this point, the Armour Home was serving residents whose families were likely living in nearby neighborhoods. The Gillis Home had developed seventy years of broad and deep connections to the greater Kansas City community. That goodwill was important. From the 1950s through the 1970s, the Gillis Home's population shifted yet again. Everywhere, there was a growing need for programs for children with special requirements. The physically or mentally disabled, the emotionally distressed children, the children who had experienced violence—these were the children needing help. Again, the Gillis Home gave its energies to include those most in distress. While many group homes face challenges as they try to fit in the surrounding communities, such was not the case in Waldo. The earliest records of the local business association make note of regular activities with Gillis. Support ranged from fundraisers by the local merchants to help in buying vans to transport the children, to the Brookside Mothers' Association painting a mural in one of the cottages.

Through more than 140 years, the Gillis Home, now simply "Gillis," has provided a home for those "most distressed," as the founders once described them. Both the Armour and Gillis Homes have remained on the Waldo campus, expanding their facilities and programs. In 1997, Gillis formed an alliance with other similar caregiving agencies, an alliance they call the Cornerstones of Care. As the industry for elder care changed, the Armour Home changed its name to Armour Oaks, built a new senior facility and converted the former space into Legacy House, an assisted living program. Most importantly, both organizations not only carry on their ties to Waldo, but also play an important role in ensuring that Waldo remains a community that embraces everyone, despite their age or need.

Waldo's Towering Landmark

Where new houses are built, there must be services. There must be shops and schools and churches. There needs to be roads for cars, gas and electrical lines for houses and police and fire service for protection. And water. Lots and lots of water.

Early photo of the water tower at Seventy-fifth Street and Holmes, which came to be known as the Waldo Tower. The tower was built in 1919. *Waldo Tower Historic Society.*

In 1919, a very busy year of growth for Waldo, the city built a water tower to serve the southeast area. The site chosen was some available property at Seventy-fifth Street and Holmes Road, owned by Frank and Grace Riley. The city paid the Rileys $14,616 for a little bit more than eight acres. As a bonus, the city named the new structure the Frank T. Riley Memorial Water Tower. It's doubtful that anyone ever really called it that, however. It's always been known as the Waldo Water Tower.

From the outset, the tower boasted two remarkable traits. What everyone noticed as they drove past was the tower's style, a curious but effective blend of several European castle elements, including crenellated roof lines, arched windows and a stucco exterior, all painted in a gleaming white. It was a handsome addition to Waldo and quickly became a community landmark. The other feature was invisible and probably of little interest to most. The tower incorporated some unique and cutting-edge technology and construction methods. Engineers of the day characterized it as one of the first and largest reinforced concrete standpipes ever attempted in America. Its base was laid in a continuous pour of concrete, which took two days. More remarkably, the tower was formed in a continuous pour of fourteen days. To accomplish this, the builders used a new technique known as "slip form" in which the concrete forms were elevated on jacks as work progressed. When finished, the tower held one million gallons. Even at that, it was intended only for high demand use. The property on which the tower sits is ideal for such use, being at one of the area's highest elevation points. Original plans called for an observation tower, but the idea proved impractical. Still, the water tower was a wonderful addition to Waldo. It quickly became a park-like gathering place for Waldo residents.

As World War II was drawing to a close and the wave of returning veterans needed assistance, Congress passed the GI Bill that extended to them a range of benefits that included housing assistance. This created an instant and very attractive market for some developers. With government backing of the loans, the risk behind the investment was minimal. A fortune could be made in volume if the developer was interested in meeting the expedient, rather than long-term need. Many were. In fairness, there was legitimate demand for housing whose tenants would only be there temporarily as they waited reassignment or discharge. Some of the housing itself might be temporary, the metal bivouac-sort built for places not normally equipped to handle residents. But some of what was built was simply shoddy, thrown together quickly and cheaply and designed to make a nice profit off a sure thing.

That's what the residences around the Waldo Water Tower feared when, in 1944, the development concern of Sachs-Fels-Straub asked the city to approve a thirty-home housing project on the ten acres directly south of and adjacent to the water tower site. They called their project Troostview and, in fact, had started a few homes on property they already owned just south of the tower site. The project had moved through first Jackson County and then city processes without objection. But just as the question was coming before the Kansas City Council, the neighborhood spoke up. They wisely chose not to oppose the housing directly, less it seem they were unwelcoming of returning veterans. Instead, they offered an alternative. Waldo wanted a park.

The park would not completely stop the housing development. The owners had already started development south of Seventy-eight Street and only wanted the remnant of property between their land and the tower site for a few more houses. The neighborhood wanted it as a buffer to the development. After some haggling over the price of the property, the city chose to side with the Waldo neighborhoods. From those first community organizing efforts, the Tower Park Homes Association was formed. A few years later, when it was time to name five new parks, the Waldo site one of them, only three suggestions were presented at the Parks Board meeting to decide the matter. One was to honor two former school principals. Another was to name each of the five parks after one of the Dionne quintuplets. Waldo resident Leo T. Schwarz had only one suggestion. The park at Seventy-fifth Street and Holmes Road should be called "Tower Park," he said, "because that is what everyone calls it."

In its first few years, improvements were made to the park and the water tower. The city erected playground equipment and built a baseball diamond. On the north face of the property, the city installed a ten-million-gallon underground reservoir and adjacent pumping station in 1938. Then, in 1957, the city decommissioned the water tower. The tower had outlived its usefulness. It had neither the capacity nor the technology to meet current demands. There was plenty of city hall wrangling over the next few years to determine whether the Parks Department or the Water Department would be responsible for the property. In the end, the park property became the purview of Parks, and the empty tower belonged to Water Services.

If the working water tower had been a source of fascination to the community, an abandoned one was even more intriguing, particularly to young people in Waldo. The city tried all the security devices imaginable to keep kids from climbing fences and scaling ladders that were off-limits. As such things often are, it was probably a rite of passage to claim to have scaled the tower and seen all the way to downtown from its top, or to claim to have seen stolen treasure or dead bodies inside, just to heighten the excitement.

So it was understandable that when some children claimed they had seen what they thought was a body at the bottom of the inside of the tower, they couldn't get anyone to believe them. According to the August 1962 newspaper accounts, the kids weren't sure themselves what they had seen, and—worried about getting into trouble—they mentioned it to no one for several days. But one girl finally spoke up to her mother, and the police were notified. When the officers reached the top of the tower, they saw that the girl had been right.

In no time, the scene was overrun with police and fire personnel. At times over the next five hours, the spectators would number in the hundreds. Officers spent most of their time keeping the crowd out of the way. The problem was that there was no way to the bottom except from the top, which could only be entered through the small arched windows that rimmed it. Those windows were too small and too high to get any kind of hauling equipment through them. For two hours, firefighters lowered grappling hooks in an effort to raise the body. Then someone from the water department remembered a manhole on the side of the tower near the base that had been used during its construction and then plastered over. Workers started chipping away at the spot until they found the cover, then a torch was used to cut off the metal cap. They broke through to the inside of the tower at three o'clock in the morning.

There they found the body of James Everett Royse. The billfold they found near the body identified him as twenty years old and living at Seventy-fifth Street and Troost Avenue. He had fallen thirteen stories inside the tower. When they contacted his mother, she said he had been missing since the prior November—nearly nine months. A friend of the boy's confirmed that he and Royse had been to the tower the night Royse disappeared. Royse had been walking home from Waldo, where he got his polio booster shot from his doctor's office. Once the young man's body was removed, the hole was replastered. The patch is still visible on the tower's western side.

The tragedy had opened many eyes to the tower's condition, and what they saw worried them. Those who worried about safety wanted the tower destroyed. Others who loved the tower for their own reasons worried that it *would* be destroyed. But the engineers, architects and construction experts worried about its condition and how long it could last before it simply crumbled. The neighborhood rallied again and, through local efforts, had the Waldo Water Tower declared a landmark of the American Waterworks Association in August 1975. Honored for those early and innovative construction practices, the tower was the association's first designation in Missouri and only its twenty-fifth throughout the country. The community effort also included the application to have the tower placed on the National Register of Historic Places. On occasion of the AWWA designation, the city held a formal ceremony in the park. Dr. Charles B. Wheeler Jr., mayor of Kansas City, represented the city in accepting the honor. Vince Bilardo's Dixie Land Band entertained the crowd.

The designations had secured that the Waldo Tower would not be deliberately torn down. Keeping it from falling down was another matter entirely. The Parks Department continued to maintain and even add features to Tower Park. Except for neighborhood complaints, there was little incentive for the Water Department to repair the tower and little in the way of money to pay for it. Advocating for its preservation remained a favorite cause in the neighborhoods, but there were always so many other needs that the tower's preservation lost out as a priority. In 2009, the community adopted a new approach. A group of neighbors collaborated in the formation of the Waldo Tower Historic Society. The tower was ninety years old by now, and it certainly had a history to tell. Its reputation as a community landmark transcended Waldo to include the entire city. And as its blighted appearance had been saying something less than favorable about the neighborhood for the last fifty years, the society members knew its shining restoration would say something positive and important to the future of the Waldo area.

Though the Waldo Tower has never been open as an observation point, engineers assessing its condition captured a view that is open to the north as far as downtown Kansas City. *Waldo Tower Historic Society.*

One of the society's first tasks was to conduct an assessment of the tower's condition. Treanor Architects was hired, and they came back with a report that was dismaying. But at least now the society knew what the tower needed. The principal threat was the exterior. The stucco was cracking and deteriorated on all sides. There was work to do around the parapet, too, as well as the roof. There was metal damage. Nature had been hard on the tower. The good news was that nothing was beyond repair. The tower could be fixed. It was only a matter of money. A lot of money. The 2010 estimate gave the repairs a sizeable price tag. But that hasn't deterred the Waldo Tower Historic Society as it continues to advocate for the repair of the tower, to raise money for the tower's restoration and to remind the community of the role that the tower has played in the history of Waldo. Because of the society's work, the last chapter in the history of the Waldo Tower has yet to be written, but it promises a happy ending.

Chapter 4

1940–1970: BIG PLANS

You can always amend a big plan, but you can never expand a little one. I don't believe in little plans. I believe in plans big enough to meet a situation which we can't possibly foresee now.
—Harry Truman

Kansas City was pulsing with an excitement it hadn't seen for twenty years. The Great Depression was over. A war raged in Europe, and while across the country there was still a debate about whether the United States would enter the war, some communities like Kansas City weren't going to wait to find out. The race to get defense contracts was on. Local leaders lobbied Washington, touting Kansas City's advantages—its central location, its rails and its ready workforce. It didn't hurt Kansas City's efforts to have Senator Harry Truman on its side or that J.C. Nichols was on the President's Advisory Council for National Defense.

The civic efforts were hugely successful. Between 1940 and 1943, the Kansas City area landed a series of industrial plums, including the Remington Arms plant in Independence, the Lake City Ordinance Plant and the North American Aviation plant in Fairfax on the Kansas side. But for Waldo and south Kansas City, the prize was the new Pratt & Whitney plant, where aircraft engines would be built. The Pratt & Whitney Plant sat near the southern end of the Dodson line. The rails were once again playing an important role in Waldo's growth.

Thanks to all that new industrial growth, there was money to spend after the long drought of the 1930s. Jobs were plentiful, and the pay was good.

City road crews pave the stretch of Wornall Road just north of Eighty-fifth Street in 1952. The city limits weren't extended this far until 1947. *Missouri Valley Special Collections, Kansas City Public Library, Kansas City, MO.*

Granted, there weren't as many ways to spend that cash, what with the constant rationing. And there were service men everywhere. Once America was formally in the war, Kansas City's Union Station handled about two hundred trains a day, transporting troops and supplies all over the nation. Some of the troops would bivouac here for a while, waiting for their final orders. The proliferation of bars, juke joints and other various amusements took Kansas City back to its Wild West days.

All this growth was heady. It fueled a sense that the future was unlimited and that Kansas City would grow indefinitely. The city made big plans for its postwar life. In 1947, the city expanded its boundaries for the first time in nearly forty years. Waldo was now fully within the city's limits. The sprawl didn't end there, and in just a few short years, Kansas City more than doubled in size from what it had been at the start of the war, more than three hundred square miles. To support all that growth, the City Council approved a major bond issue to fund nearly $50 million in improvements. The plans were for new community centers, more parks, repairs to the bridges and updates to the airport. But most of the

An unidentified young woman helps promote Waldo in Kansas City's Centennial Parade, held downtown in 1950. *Betty Tillotson.*

money was for transportation. Streets were needed now for the postwar automobile generation. The streetcar lines were fine, but a car was within almost everyone's economic reach and offered so much freedom.

No one really argued that all this growth was bad. But across the city, neighborhoods and business interests were organizing and making plans of their own. In the subtlest of ways, the city began to splinter into smaller units. New communities—suburbs—were popping up in the span of just a few years, and some neighborhoods that had been around for years were

This 1960 aerial view of the intersection of Eighty-fifth Street and Wornall Road (center) shows the city's recently acquired Sunnyside Park (center bottom), as well as the extent of development to the south. *Wilborn & Associates.*

finally incorporating as cities. Among others, Leawood, Prairie Village and Roeland Park on the Kansas side, as well as Gladstone and Riverside on the Missouri side, all incorporated between 1948 and 1952. New neighborhoods sharpened the competition for homebuyers, for shoppers and for critical public dollars. Waldo was no different. The businesses in Waldo would make their own plans. They were determined not to be forgotten in the heat of competition—or run over in the frenzy of growth.

THE HOME OF FRIENDLY MERCHANTS

Around 1905, David Proctor formed the Waldo-Westmoreland Improvement Association. His reasons may have been simply that Proctor owned property in Waldo and wanted to develop it. It was a relatively small piece of property off the northeast corner of Seventy-fifth Street and Broadway. Coincidentally, it was part of David Waldo's original holdings, so in that sense, it was in the very heart of Waldo. But Proctor was starting out exactly at the same time as J.C. Nichols, so perhaps he watched Nichols to learn how this business of real estate development was done. In forming the association, Proctor's only goal might have been to give his development more gravitas. But the fact that twenty years later, the Waldo-Westmoreland Improvement Association was being credited with much of Waldo's success suggests Proctor had a vision that a business association could mean much more to Waldo's future.

For centuries, chambers of commerce have been promoting the businesses of their members. Starting early in the twentieth century, a new twist was added. Business associations didn't just promote their members. This new breed saw business as a critical part of the community. Business associations welcomed membership from any property owner, business operator or organization with an interest in community's welfare. They used the clout of their commercial status at city hall to advocate for or against issues of broader interest. They worked with the neighborhoods around them. In short, they promoted place over commerce, in the belief that a strong community would make for strong businesses. The Nichols Company was a big proponent of the idea. In addition to establishing neighborhood associations throughout the Country Club District, Nichols established merchant associations at each of their commercial sites, staffed, managed and largely funded by the company.

In 1925, the Waldo-Westmoreland Improvement Association would not have had such corporate largess to support its organization. Its support came only from the Waldo community, and that seemed to be enough. In a 1925 article on Waldo in the magazine the *City Ice Man*, long-time Waldo resident and businessman S.D. Slaughter commented on the association's legacy:

> *We old-timers recognized that we had many things to accomplish before we could rank even as a village. There were streets to be made, sidewalks to be laid, streets to light and churches and schools to build. Feeling the need of all these things, we perfected the organization that even to this day, operates under the name of the Waldo-Westmoreland Improvement Association. From its humble beginnings this organization, which has been in existence for more than twenty years, now enjoys a membership*

of over 150 members. This little association carefully laid plans for a beautiful little city. They have witnessed these plans materialize and have seen their fondest dreams fulfilled.

Yet for all the apparent success, the Waldo-Westmoreland Improvement Association did not last. The reasons for its demise are lost in history, though it's likely that the long, hard times of the 1930s stripped away the manpower, the interest and the money to do its work. But now, in 1940, a new association emerged—the Southwest Business Association.

The Southwest Business Association was chartered in 1940. The early records of the association have not survived. What records do exist begin with the June 1955 minutes of its monthly meeting. After fifteen years of operation, those minutes reveal an organization with a small membership struggling to gather momentum. The first year of records covers numerous discussions on ways to get more business owners to join and come to the meetings. But by 1959, the membership numbers were up to 150. The group was finally gaining traction, as well as gaining a reputation in Kansas City as an organization making big plans.

Waldo had plenty to plan for. In the 1950s, Kansas City was making public investment at a rate rivaling the 1920s. In Waldo, that meant that now, the whole stretch of Wornall Road would be paved. It meant that the city finally acquired all of the old Sunnyside Dairy property next to the Gillis and Armour Homes for a beautiful new park. The school district proudly opened George Caleb Bingham Junior High School at Seventy-sixth and Wyandotte Streets. But not all the news was good. In 1957, the streetcar line closed. For the first time in more than half a century, there was no train you could ride in and out of Waldo. The automobile had finally defeated the rails.

Waldo was surrounded by competition. Every new housing development had its own shiny new retail center, where all the buildings were neat and uniform, and there was plenty of parking. Not so in Waldo. The remnants of its industrial days were everywhere, from the ramshackle buildings that dotted Wornall Road, to the nearly abandoned railroad tracks. Waldo was anything but neat or uniform. The fact that it had only recently been annexed didn't help. The city was developing ordinances to regulate signage, building codes and parking in many neighborhoods. But places on the city's fringe, like Waldo, were not high on the city's priority list.

By the early 1960s, the Southwest Business Association had stabilized into a well-respected community organization. Its monthly meetings were on the regular lunch circuit for every elected and appointed public official in Kansas City. People in Waldo could get the attention of city hall when they needed to. Influence drew membership and, with that, the involvement of more businesses for events and promotions. It was at this time that the Southwest Business Association made three strategic choices that proved critical to Waldo's fight for the market.

One strategy was promotional. The Southwest Business Association changed its name to the Waldo Area Business Association in 1964. In the 1960s, when anything "new" seemed to be the rage, Waldo promoted against the stereotype. The association focused on the traditional and the familiar and the value in what they had always offered—the satisfaction of dealing with businesses that had stood the test of time, a place that was familiar and friendly. The association chose a new slogan and emblazoned it on the twenty-foot sign the association had built near Seventy-fifth Street and Wornall Road. "Waldo," it proclaimed in electrified in letters six feet high, "The Home of Friendly Merchants."

As if to show off its friendly nature, Waldo started promoting itself within its ranks and beyond its borders. Waldo was everywhere—represented in parades, participating in charity functions and out in force supporting the new baseball franchise, the Royals. There were more functions, more promotions and more committees than ever before. The Waldo Area Business Association was able to pull all this off and more, thanks to the help of their executive secretary, Ruth Bradfield. The association hired its first employee in 1959, but a year later, they also hired Ruth Bradfield. Ruth was a perfect choice. She was a notary insurance agent with an office right in the heart of Waldo. For the next twenty-five years, Ruth Bradfield kept the association's books, paid its bills, took the minutes and attended to all the details of the association. To honor her memory, a small park next to the transit stop at Seventy-sixth Street and Wornall Road was named for her in 1984.

The second strategy was the formation of the Waldo Progress Committee, charged with getting Waldo into the modern age as far as development was concerned. Waldo would need an area plan, a public policy device to organize and regulate development. But when city hall claimed to have no money for the effort, folks in Waldo were typically undeterred. The Waldo Progress Committee took on the project itself. Its members did all the legwork, including drafting a zoning map, conducting a traffic count, compiling an inventory of property owners and conducting an assessment of Waldo's parking capacity. It took some months before the Progress Committee finished its work, but when it did, the committee

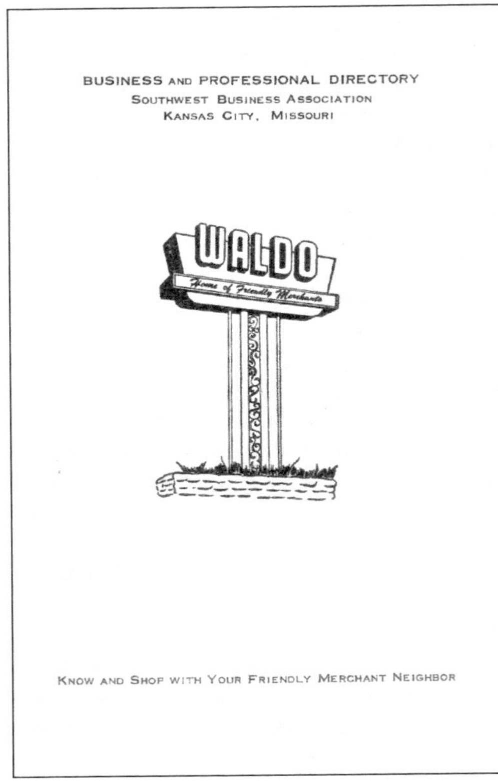

Right: The local business association was still known as the Southwest Business Association when it published one of its first member directories, which featured the iconic Waldo sign that once stood near Seventy-fifth Street and Wornall Road. *Waldo Area Business Association.*

Below: Ruth Bradfield served more than twenty years as the business association's staff person. Here she organizes name tags for one of the group's monthly luncheons. *Waldo Area Business Association.*

presented the City Plan Commission with its findings. The city took several years to respond, but eventually, in 1969, Waldo got its plan.

The city's plan was big, bold and would, if it was completed, bring a drastic change to Waldo. It could all be summed up in the fanciful illustration at the center of the city's report, the city's vision for Waldo. In the drawing, Wornall Road was transformed into a highly landscaped trench where both cars and light rail traveled thirty feet below street level. People strolled casually down sidewalks that ran between the transportation trench and quaint shops that resembled the existing buildings. The problem was, the existing buildings would have to disappear to make room for what the city called the "improvements."

Though the plan had some supporters in Waldo, overall, Waldo locals generally dismissed the proposal. There might have been more concern except for the fact that the city was clear on one point—there would be no money to build this ambitious project any time soon. Still, the plan as a city policy would keep Waldo's future up in the air. The years ahead would force the Waldo Area Business Association to work hard and to constantly think of new approaches if it wanted to survive such uncertainty.

A Long, Thin Ribbon of Rail

In 1957, the last streetcar line in Kansas City made its final run. It was the Country Club Line—No. 56—the line that served Brookside and Waldo. The most popular of the city's transit lines, the Country Club Line held on long after the other routes were closed. But the Kansas City Public Service Company, the franchise operators, had been struggling for some time. The truth that few wanted to acknowledge was that the streetcars never really turned much of a profit, and the system had been steadily losing ridership since the early 1920s, when the automobile first appeared. That was the decade when the Public Service Company started augmenting their streetcar service with bus service. Over the years, any time the city tried to impose an assessment on the company for the maintenance cost of its rails running in the streets, the Public Service Company would pull up its tracks and run a bus line instead.

To those faithful riders of the Country Club Line, the passing of the streetcar was a sad day, a sign that times were changing. To the businesses

One of the last runs of the Country Club Streetcar line, as it pulls into the Waldo Station area from the south, circa 1955. *Wilborn & Associates.*

that had relied for so long on the streetcar trade to help bolster sales, the passing was less about nostalgia than simple economics. Ironically, the closing of the line might offer a chance for Waldo to get something it needed now more than ever—parking lots. In true Waldo form, the merchants started working with the city, as owners of the railroad right-of-way, on turning the Waldo streetcar station area at Seventy-fifth Street and Broadway into a parking lot. This seemed, at first, to be a simple request. But Waldo walked into a hornet's nest that plagued it for years and left it tied up by a long, thin ribbon of rail.

Back in the early 1900s when J.C. Nichols bought the old Westport Railway and sold it back to the Metropolitan Street Railway Company for the bargain-basement price of $15,000, he had two conditions. The first was that the line be electrified, which the Met (as the railway company was known) did willingly. The second was that the Met terminate any freight operation on the line. Nichols certainly didn't want noisy, smelly freight trains scuttling through his upscale neighborhoods. On this point, the Met declined, forfeiting an additional $50,000 that Nichols had pledged on satisfying his conditions. In so doing, the Met inadvertently caused a legal split of the easement, or right-of-way, which ran with the tracks. One easement went to the Met, and over the years to the various iterations of the franchise operators, culminating with the Kansas City Public Service Company that operated the system at the time the streetcars stopped. The other easement went to the newly formed Kansas City Public Freight Company, a separate franchise that the city granted for freight service on the line.

Nichols's concerns for his own neighborhoods were allayed. He got what he wanted, because freight traffic slowly ceased north of Gregory Boulevard. But the question of the right-of-way lingered in the background of Nichols's Country Club District for years, until the late 1950s. At that time, the city began to discuss using the right-of-way as the basis for a major freeway project that, when completed, would have connected the north and south stretches of the federal interstate loop that would one day encircle the metropolitan area. The plan seemed modern and had the backing of prominent Kansas City interests, including the Nichols Company. The first opposition came from some of the residents of the northern stretch whose homes abutted the easement. They fought the city for a number of reasons and, in so doing, raised the awareness of homeowners in the whole area. The road that proponents were calling the "Country Club Freeway," would have laid waste to several blocks on either side of both Brookside Boulevard and Wornall Road from the Plaza south to where the freeway would run near 103rd Street. Early plans showed the road would run below grade at places, effectively isolating neighborhoods on one side from the other, except for a bridge over the road every mile or so.

Two things kept the road from being built. Ultimately, the Missouri Department of Transportation, the lead agency on the project, walked away from the continued delays on the freeway at that location. The state chose instead to pursue a route farther to the east where neighborhood opposition wasn't as organized or powerful. Thirty years later, that road became Bruce R. Watkins Drive, an extension of 71 Highway. But the delays weren't caused by conflict with the neighborhoods. They had merely slowed the process down long enough for the courts to get involved. When the Kansas City Public Service Company ceased to exist as a franchise in 1957, the city took control of the company's assets, including—they believed—the streetcar right-of-way. But there were several disputes over which entity owned the property or had a claim to the easement, disputes that took more than one case to local and state courts. Ultimately, the courts ruled that the city lacked clear authority to condemn what had been public property to begin with. So for now, the freeway project was closed. But if there was no longer a Kansas City Public Service Company, there was a vestige of the old freight company. In 1957, the freight company was bought and reformed as the Kansas City Public Service Freight Operation, under the ownership of James Ashley Sr.

At first, these wranglings were of no interest to the Waldo Area Business Association. As most people did, the association started out with the assumption that the city controlled the easement, a stretch of property some eight miles long but only about one hundred feet wide. The association's lawyer was also a city councilman—Charles Shafer Jr. With Shafer's help, Waldo negotiated an agreement with the city to use the old Waldo station near Seventy-fifth Street and Wornall Road. It was built in 1907 to power the newly electrified lines. Over the years, space had been added to accommodate waiting passengers. In its heyday it housed a lunchroom and a big Coca-Cola sign that hung on the side of the building. The streetcars would pull in front, but there was extra track for turnarounds and switching of cars to accommodate the freight trains that ran as far as Gregory Boulevard. The station made the area the center of Waldo. Now it would have to be torn down to accommodate the parking lot.

The business association signed a lease with the city and charged rent to the surrounding businesses that benefited most directly from the improvement. There were always grumblings about the charges, but there was little doubt that the additional parking was essential to Waldo's future success. But when the city's plan for a freeway along the right-of-way came up, the whole question of the property rights came to the fore. The City of Kansas City started its fight to claim the right-of-way, and the Kansas City Public Service Freight Operation fought to maintain its rights to the rails.

The freight operation's claims didn't stop the city from forging ahead with its plans. The long-awaited Waldo Area Plan that the Waldo Progress Committee had worked so diligently toward was finally presented to the community in 1969. A key component of the plan was an elaborate drawing that depicted Wornall Road as being replaced, gouged out by a sleek new roadway and highly modern transit line. It was the Country Club Freeway all over again, this time adding rapid transit.

The concept had its proponents and detractors within the Waldo community. There would be a cost, of course. Houses and businesses would have to be demolished. Some considered the idea with horror, but others tried to calculate what such a plan could mean for their own bottom lines. The minutes of the Waldo Area Business Association do not record that the

From the interior of the Colormax Paint Store on Wornall Road, the Waldo streetcar station is visible. In the background are the shops on Broadway across the tracks from the station. *Wilborn & Associates.*

organization ever took an official position on the issue, but active members of the association were quoted in newspaper stories, voicing opinions on both sides.

The association's main concern, understandably, was the lack of certainty the situation caused. They had a lease for a parking lot that was constantly being called into question. The original 1958 lease was substituted for a lease with Ashley's freight operation in the mid-1960s. The city formed a separate transportation authority in 1965, and by 1974, it was again exercising its claim to the right-of-way. So Waldo signed a lease with the new agency, the Area Transportation Authority. Three years later, the freight operation's interests prevailed, and the lease was reassigned.

The ongoing legal disputes between the ATA and the Public Service Freight operation weren't the only cause for confusion, but they were the main one. In 1970, James Ashley Sr. died, but the fight was taken up by

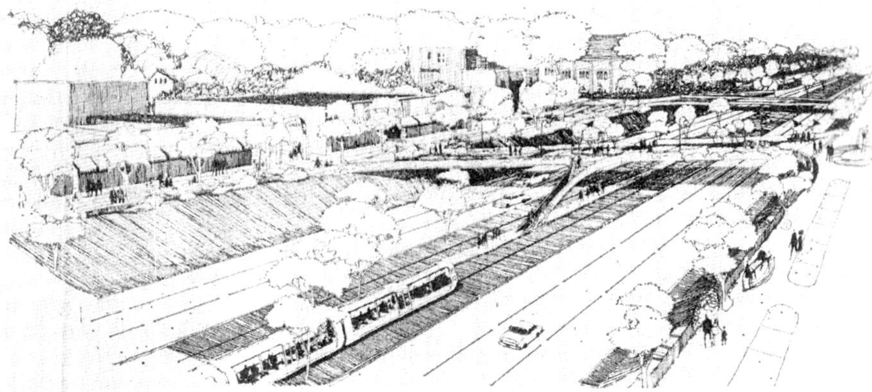

The city's 1969 plan for a midtown freeway envisioned Wornall Road replaced by a freeway below grade that could also accommodate light rail. *Waldo Area Business Association.*

Ashley's son, James Ashley Jr. The dispute that had begun in 1962 with the formation of the Kansas City Public Service Freight Operation didn't finally resolve itself until the arguments were heard by both the Interstate Commerce Commission and the Missouri Supreme Court. The city had started out with a tentative agreement with the Ashley family for the rights for a mere $30,000 in 1965. By 1980, the Ashleys were rejecting an offer by the city of more than $4 million, made possible by a federal grant. With the rejection, the grant fell through. Just a year later, the matter was finally resolved, and the Ashleys were awarded $2.5 million.

Ironically, the sticking point was the Ashley family's commitment to the idea of light rail transit over freeways. Later newspaper accounts quoted James Ashley Jr. as saying, "My idea all along has been to preserve [the right-of-way] for the use of mass transit. We'd work together with [the city.]" After the fuel crisis of the 1970s, the city was on board with mass transit, too. But just because the city and the freight operation had come to terms didn't mean the matter was resolved. There were dozens of individual property owners adjacent to the track that contended that they had a claim to the right-of-way. This was a situation the city couldn't afford to tolerate. If it ever hoped to see light rail along those tracks, there could be no question of rights. If these numerous individual property owners were given rights and made any sort of improvements on the property, it would be cost prohibitive for the city to acquire the property in the future. That would make any future transit project impossible.

For another ten years, the city fought individual and collective lawsuits to preserve the rights for which it had paid so dearly. The last lawsuit was kicked out of the courts in 1994, and the ATA finally had clear claim to the right-of-way. But now, the interest in light rail was wavering. Gas prices were stable and relatively low. Kansas Citians continued to enjoy the independence the car gave them and saw no reason to give that up. Urban core neighborhoods like Brookside and Waldo generally liked the idea of light rail, but they also generally disliked the idea of living next to it. Still, the city wanted to maintain its options.

The old tracks were an eyesore and a hazard. Now long since unused, the easement was blighted. The tracks were covered with weeds, and the rails laid loosely on an unstable bed. On some stretches, the rail was a favorite spot for illegal dumping. In places where it was used for parking, like Brookside and Waldo, the shopping areas struggled to maintain the property despite the rents they paid to the ATA. Working with the neighborhood and business groups along the route, the ATA developed a plan that was widely embraced. The rails were removed, to be replaced with a walking and biking trail that would connect everything between the Plaza and Dodson, just as the streetcars had once done. Upon dedication in 1996, the trail was named the Harry Wiggins Trolley Track Trail, in honor of the local state senator whose support had been instrumental in getting the project funded. Over the years, the Trolley Track Trail has served as neighborhood connector, community gathering point and the route of area charity races. And in the event that the mass transit issue is ever resolved locally, it retains its capacity to serve that way, too.

A Carnival Atmosphere

There's something about a place that lives on the fringe of civilization. Such a place will develop habits and customs that straddle the rules, be they rules of state or society. The habits are not always developed out of defiance, though there is always that element. Sometimes, it's simply that for those on the fringe, there's so much uncertainty about which rules apply that they tend to make up their own rules. For everyone else, the problems of the city at its edges are remote concerns.

Waldo spent its first one hundred years on the fringe. First it was on the fringe of the frontier, then on the border of the Union, then at the edge

Riders wave as the Kiddieland train takes off for a run around the park, while a car speeding down Wornall Road seems to give chase. *Wilborn & Associates.*

of the city. To some this might have seemed a problem, but not for the businesses of Waldo. They saw that there were many markets for a fringe trade. Waldo had already profited in areas other communities would have shunned, like the railroad, the lumberyards and the grain mills. And now there were "amusements." Starting in the 1940s, Waldo became known as a place to go and have fun. And in this regard, Waldo's most famous and enduring amusement was Kiddieland Park.

The Kansas City area has had a long love affair with amusement parks. The courtship began in the 1880s, with picnic parks on the outskirts of the city on all sides, from Independence on the east to Shawnee on the west. The trolley car companies created these parks as places where the urban dwellers could take a day trip, enjoy lunch by a pond in the shade and fill their lungs with fresh air and their faces with warm sunshine. But when electricity arrived, the nature of these parks changed and so did their location. They moved into the city, not away from it, close to the sources of power. These parks sparkled with water during the hot summer days and with light on the hot summer nights. Kansas City's most famous and long-lived of these, Electric Park, opened in 1907. At Forty-seventh Street and The Paseo Boulevard, Electric Park was not so terribly far from Waldo, and it was built the same year that Waldo saw its first real development. Fairyland Park was not so far from Waldo, either. Built in 1923 on the city's southeastern corner of Seventy-fifth Street and Prospect Avenue, Fairyland arrived just two years before Electric Park closed. After that, Fairyland Park became *the* park for the area until it closed in 1977, after a struggle over the admittance of blacks and years of declining revenue. The revenue had declined mostly because, north of the river, Worlds of Fun opened in 1973, Kansas City's modern "theme" park. Worlds of Fun obliterated any competition.

But in the late forties and early fifties, in the classic era of returning soldiers and burgeoning young families, another sort of park emerged. The Kiddieland phenomenon was not confined to Kansas City. In fact, the term "kiddieland" is a term of the amusement park industry that specifically identifies small-scale parks designed to attract visitors from a few miles' radius, and to cater to families with small children. The parks themselves fit neatly in the corners of commercial areas, and at first, they were supported by surrounding merchants because they drew customers to the area. Kiddieland might have been small, but it had all the components of any good park—a roller coaster, a merry-go-round, a ferris wheel and an ice cream stand. There were at least two Kiddieland parks in the area, one in Mission, Kansas, and the other in Waldo at the northwest corner of Eighty-fifth Street and Wornall Road.

Before Kiddieland was built on that site, there had been a combination pony ring and miniature golf course called Vaughn Kearley's Pony Go-Round. But when Kiddieland opened in 1951, it billed itself as having "every modern ride for the kiddies." The ponies stayed for a while, but the real draw was the mechanical rides. They were real rides, not miniature, and kids of all ages did in fact ride them. But the size of the property—between five and six acres—meant the rides were scaled down. These attractions might seem tame by later standards, but each ride was designed to evoke childhood fantasies shared by all. You could pretend to ride in a train, or drive a car, or steer a boat. You could ride into the past on the "Prairie Schooner" or into the future on the "Sky Fighter." And while it was only feet, not stories, above the ground, the Little Dipper roller coaster gave plenty of thrills as it clanged and banged around its tracks.

Local favorite Country Club Dairy provided Kiddieland's frozen treats, an attraction that children of all ages could enjoy. *Wilborn & Associates.*

The good times rarely last, although before it was all over, Kiddieland served Waldo and the area for more than a decade. Ultimately, the park couldn't compete with Fairyland, which had its own Kiddieland. Zoning ordinances were changing, and parks that were once considered neighborhood assets were now nuisances. These parks were increasingly expensive to operate and more vulnerable to all sorts of liabilities. The day of the small, independent park operation was fading. Kiddieland closed down in 1963, and the property was cleared for a new shopping center.

Bars and nightclubs are another of the businesses that live on the fringe, and over the years, Waldo has had its share. In fact, it was during the 1950s and '60s that Waldo gained its reputation as a popular nightspot. Until 1947, everything south of Seventy-seventh Street in Waldo was still outside the city limits. With no liquor control officers, lots of little taverns and roadhouses opened up along south Wornall Road. By the time the city boundaries were extended to Eighty-fifth Street, Waldo's reputation and trade were well established. A 1947 *Kansas City Star* article, likely prompted by the recent annexation, talked about the character of the area, describing it as a place "where a night life zone of beer joints, hamburger stands, filling stations, vegetable stands and egg and milk shops has grown up along Wornall Road from Seventy-fifth to Eighty-fifth streets. Until the city extended its limits… this was a no man's land, governed only by deputy sheriffs, whose regime never was too severe."

One of the most notorious joints was a place simply called "Mary's." Mary started in a wood shack at 8007 Wornall Road, where it's been said that she used gimmicks like women's wrestling matches to attract customers. Later, she built a brick building at 7837 Wornall, with a second floor where Mary reportedly lived. There were plenty of other joints that came and went over the years—places with classic names like The Mayfair, The Stoplight Tavern, Buster's Roxy Inn and Tootie Clarkin's Dance Dine and Drink Emporium. The good times rolled in Waldo through the late 1970s. But a small share of the local haunts were moving in a direction that crossed a

Zepi's was one of the area's first pizza parlors. This songbook allowed patrons to sing along with the player piano, while advising those new to the experience that "Pizza is eaten with the fingers!" *LaDene Morton.*

line for the neighborhoods. The local paper called them clubs with "go-go dancers," but it was a euphemism for strip clubs. Neighbors and businesses alike signed petitions to stop the trend, and they won. Waldo bars might be dives, but at least now they were decent dives.

Waldo also had a growing reputation for good food. Some of Waldo's popular restaurants featured evocative names designed to reach beyond the regular ambience of Waldo—names like Mancuso's Gondola Restaurant and Lounge, the Desert Inn, and The Last Resort. Some names sounded more like neighborhood haunts—the Chew & Chat, Pearl's Lunch and the Hot Cake House. Trillin's on Gregory Boulevard, a favorite spot for the meetings of the business association in the 1950s, was owned by Abe Trillin, father of Waldo's most famous son, author Calvin Trillin. Waldo's most famous restaurant was also one of Kansas City's. Jasper Mirabile opened Jasper's Restaurant on the southwest corner of Seventy-fifth Street and Wornall Road in 1954 as a small neighborhood Italian restaurant. Over the decade, Jasper's evolved into a world-class establishment, and it was a popular place for visiting celebrities to dine. In 1978, Jasper's was the first Kansas City restaurant to receive the highly regarded Mobil Four Star rating. The Waldo tradition of great joints and good times was formalized in 2003 when the

Waldo continues as a favorite watering spot. Here, patrons of The Well enjoy a visit from the world-famous Clydesdales. *Waldo Area Business Association.*

Waldo Area Business Association organized the first Waldo pub-crawl. The pub-crawl shuttles patrons between participating bars and restaurants, and it is one of the association's best methods of promoting Waldo. In the past decade, the semiannual Waldo pub-crawls have cemented Waldo's image as one of Kansas City's favorite entertainment districts.

Faith in Waldo

Since early in the nineteenth century, local houses of worship of all stripes have been central to the Waldo's growth and its sense of community. Their sanctuaries have provided stability to development and to the people of Waldo. Their ranks have included congregations, parishes and temples in some of the most beautiful buildings in the area. But there are four churches that began in Waldo's humbler digs, in settings that weren't very church-like at all.

Waldo's first known church began its life as the Waldo Sunday School in 1907. The first fundraiser was held at the blacksmith's shop on Seventy-fifth Street, just west of Wornall Road. Neighbors made donations for the privilege of coming in to listen to a gramophone play a recording of the great Caruso. Later that year, when Pitkin Hall was built next door, it served as the first meeting place for the church. By the end of that first year, the church was officially chartered as Broadway Methodist Episcopal Church. Within the next year, the congregation had built its first sanctuary at Seventy-fourth Street and Wornall Road on property owned by one of its members. Through expansions and changes, it has remained there since, but it is now known as Broadway United Methodist Church.

The Broadway Church was nearly alone in Waldo for its first ten years. In 1917, Waldo area Catholics met with the local bishop to advocate for a Waldo parish. In a few short months, the newly created St. Elizabeth Parish began its life in a rented Waldo storefront. Its journey to a more permanent home would be a test of faith. The parish would meet in that storefront for more than a decade. While the sanctuary's exterior structure was complete in 1922, because of the Great Depression, it took another thirteen years to finish the interior. The delay allowed for the addition of a bell tower, so at the church's dedication ceremony in 1935, the church's new bells rang out loud.

Broadway Methodist Church at Seventy-fourth Street and Wornall Road is Waldo's oldest church, dating from 1907. *Missouri Valley Special Collections, Kansas City Public Library, Kansas City, MO.*

The Catholic community in Waldo grew so quickly that soon a second parish was needed. Christ the King Parish, at Eighty-fifth Street and Wornall Road, started out serving the growing number of Catholic families south of Waldo. Founded in 1938 to initially serve just seventeen nearby families, the parish's first home was a few blocks west of its present location on Eighty-fifth Street, in a rented storeroom. A few weeks later, it moved to a nearby tin barn, but when a passerby mistook it for a tavern, a cross was hastily attached to the barn. Just three years later, with more than four times the original membership, the parish built its first sanctuary in the architectural style of the Spanish missions. That sanctuary burned to the ground just two years later. Situated outside the city, there was no fire protection service to save it. The parishioners managed to rebuild the church exactly as it had been before in only seven months. Continued growth eventually rendered that building obsolete for the parish's needs, and the present church was built in 1952.

When erected in 1941, the main sanctuary of Christ the King Parish was built in a traditional Spanish mission style. *Wilborn & Associates.*

One building has been home to several denominations, though its origins had nothing to do with worship. The red brick building at 7100 Main Street, just south of Gregory Boulevard, started its life as home for the Kansas City Telephone Company's exchange for all lines with a "Jackson" prefix. The telephone exchange operated between 1925 and 1935, when the building was taken over by the Brookside Methodist Episcopal Church. By 1945, that church had changed its name to the Brookside Methodist Church. Another decade would pass before it became the home of the Armour Hills Branch of the Church of Jesus Christ of Latter Day Saints. And yet another decade would pass before its current worshipers moved in. In 1966, the building became known as the New Reform Temple, with ninety-eight charter members who practice Classic Reform Judaism.

Chapter 5

1970–2010: SITTING IN THE SHADE

Someone's sitting in the shade today
because someone planted a tree a long time ago.
—Warren Buffett

America's landscape has been permanently scarred by an almost invisible enemy. The scarring took years to reach Kansas City, but it was among the most damaged places in the country. The enemy was Dutch elm disease, a tiny fungus carried by a beetle a quarter-inch long. It came to the United States in the 1920s from Europe. It attacked the American elm, a tree that once grew in abundance from the Atlantic coast to the edge of the Great Plains, a tree that was favored by urban neighborhoods for its deep shade and hardiness. It took thirty years for the disease to migrate to the area. The first local reports of infection appeared in 1957. The decimation was slow but thorough. Kansas City hired a new Parks director in 1962 specifically for his experience in fighting the disease. He had some success, but after a few years, there simply wasn't enough in the city budget to pay for the large-scale inoculation that was required to defeat the disease. It was cheaper to just cut the infected trees down. By the early 1970s, some seventy thousand of Kansas City's beautiful elm trees that were so much a part of its famed parks and boulevard aesthetic were gone.

With the decimation over, by the 1970s, Kansas City had larger and more important projects in which to invest. Public and private ventures popped up everywhere, including Mid-Continent International (now

Before the great blight hit in the 1950s and '60s, much of Waldo, including this stretch of Wornall Road near Seventy-fifth Street, was lined with beautiful shading elm trees. *Dave and Bette Smith.*

Kansas City International) Airport, the Truman Sports Complex, Kemper Arena, Westport, the River Quay and Worlds of Fun. Kansas City was well positioned as the great "new" American city when it hosted the Republican National Convention in 1976. But this was just the peak before the drop in the coming roller-coaster ride. The trough of the late 1970s' energy crisis, the economic expansion of the 1980s, the burst of the real estate bubble in the 1990s and all the lesser highs and lows in between created a lot of work for communities. Trying to keep on top of challenges and not miss the chance to grab opportunities put organizations like the Waldo Area Business Association into overdrive.

At first, the challenges in Waldo far outweighed the opportunities. There was the ongoing struggle for maintenance of the parking lots, even as the ownership of those lots was in question. Waldo spent much of the 1970s trying to work with the city on mundane matters such as sign ordinances and zoning regulations and in combating nuisances like strip clubs. But for every supporter of change, there was always someone who had a vested interest in maintaining the status quo. Progress was made, but it was slow, incremental and didn't always fully address the issues at hand.

Then there was the media. Waldo businesses continued to enjoy a favorable opinion in the community, but the Waldo area, particularly the Wornall "strip" seemed to come up more frequently in stories in the local papers as an example of how the city shouldn't look. There were plenty of photographs of Wornall Road with the visual clutter of inconsistent and unkempt signs, utility poles and traffic. The loss of the elm trees that once lined Wornall Road seemed to lay bare an ugliness that hadn't been noticeable before. An article in the *Town Squire Magazine*, written by local broadcaster and columnist Walt Bodine, under the title "The Good, the Bad and the Ugly," called Wornall Road "the ugliest street in the world."

Built in the 1930s, the home of Pappas (originally Land) Chevrolet stood on the southeast corner of Gregory Boulevard and Wyandotte until it was destroyed by a fire in the 1980s. *Wilborn & Associates.*

For the next ten years, Waldo would counter each disparaging media piece with its own upbeat news. One article talked about Waldo as Kansas City's antique shop district. Another entitled "Waldo Cleans Up Its Act" profiled local businesses that had moved in or made major improvements to their stores. The title question of another feature, "What is Waldo's Secret?" gave the answer as local, friendly merchants and a neighborhood atmosphere. Finally, all the efforts of the businesses and the association started paying off. More and more the good news seemed to outweigh the bad. *Boulevard*, a popular magazine of the time that followed local entertainment, said it plainly in its 1985 piece on Waldo. "At long last, Waldo is hot!"

What followed was a robust period of development, in the investment-rich era of the 1990s. On the public side, there was the Trolley Track Trail and new gateway markers at Seventy-fifth and Eighty-fifth Streets that let everyone know they were in Waldo. On the private side, there seemed to be new businesses everywhere, even if it meant the loss of some familiar spots. A spate of local and national franchise operations settled in Waldo during this time. The Waldo Area Business Association started working on constructing a fountain next to the marker at Seventy-fifth Street, a feature that had long been planned but for which there was no money. To provide the needed endowment, the association created a new promotion—a fake mayoral election that would serve as a fundraiser. The Waldo Mayoral Race allowed those who worked or lived in Waldo to run for mayor, with the title going to the person who raised the most money for the fountain fund. The business association even tried starting its own Loan Development Company, seeding money to help businesses move into, expand or just stay in Waldo. The association had far outgrown its old management approach. Ruth Bradfield was no longer there, and despite several attempts to find others who could replace her as executive secretary, it was apparent to everyone that something more was needed.

In 1993, the Waldo Area Business Association turned to the Southtown Council. Southtown was an organization started ten years earlier by businesses and institutions north and east of Waldo, principally along Troost Avenue. But Southtown's membership wasn't limited to that area and included influential organizations like the University of Missouri–Kansas City, Research Hospital and the national headquarters of the Church of the Nazarene. Southtown had quickly gained a reputation for being effective in dealing with problems of blight, crime and waning public investment. And Southtown had capacity. They had full-time staff, a

The Waldo Fountain at Seventy-fifth Street and Wornall Road was built as a result of the fundraising efforts of the annual "Waldo Mayor" campaign. *Waldo Area Business Association.*

permanent office and a network of connections that could benefit Waldo. The two organizations had worked together on projects of mutual interest in the past, and so the idea of a professional alliance seemed logical. Waldo contracted with the Southtown Council for professional management and quickly saw the benefits.

For the next decade, Waldo began to successfully tackle more and more projects. In the late 1990s, the Brookside Business Association also contracted with Southtown for management. After that, the organizational capacity of all three groups grew exponentially. In 2000, the Brookside group took advantage of legislation that had been recently passed by the State of Missouri that allowed the formation of community improvement districts. Such districts, known as CIDs, allowed districts to levy taxes within their borders solely for the district's benefit, pending approval of property owners and residents. Brookside was confined to just a few blocks and controlled by a small number of property owners. Its road to the creation of the Brookside CID was relatively smooth. Waldo watched with interest and decided that a community improvement district would work for them, too. But creating the Waldo CID was a bigger battle. There were more than two hundred individual property owners within the Waldo CID's defined boundaries of commercial properties along Wornall Road and Gregory Boulevard. Many of the parcels were handled in trust, the remnants of the estate of deceased owners whose children no longer lived in the area. Waldo also had more corporate entities whose approval had to be gathered, entities with headquarters far from Kansas City.

It took nearly five years of canvassing, petitioning and preparation before Waldo could finally form the Waldo Community Improvement District. Since that time, Waldo has invested in providing a consistent level of maintenance and security for the entire area. The Waldo Fountain, now built, had its endowment, and the annual "Waldo Mayoral Race" now raises funds for local charities. The CID revenues allowed the district to expand its promotions, staffing, advertising and events. Because of the

Each year, the Waldo Area Business Association sponsors a Fall Festival in the heart of Waldo, drawing visitors to Waldo from all over the metro. *Waldo Area Business Association.*

CID, the Waldo Area Business Association now had fiscal security that it had never known before. The CID is effectively the planting of a tree that should provide shade for Waldo generations to come.

The canopies of elms that once lined Wornall Road, Gregory Boulevard and all the neighborhood streets that join them are long gone. But over the years, the legacy of the people and the businesses that planted themselves in Waldo is a unique community that has survived and thrived despite everything that wars, disease, depressions and sprawl threw in its path. These people and these businesses are too numerous to recount every story and do it justice. But there are two stories that can serve to demonstrate how one parcel of land or a single person can embody what Waldo represents—enterprise, community and longevity.

Silver Screens and Curtain Calls—The Waldo Theatre Building

In every community that endures as Waldo has, there is inevitably a shop, a corner, a place that provided a central experience, a definition of what it was like to grow up there. Such places are often a curious mixture of the familiar and the exotic. There is something both thrilling and comforting in knowing that just around the corner, adventure, excitement and entertainment are all waiting. In Waldo, that place was the Waldo Theatre.

The building that housed the Waldo Theatre was constructed in 1924, on the northwest corner of Seventy-fifth and Washington Streets. Though the Waldo Theatre sign hung prominently from the brick structure's corner, the building housed much more than the movie house. A drug store, a ladies dress shop and a small market filled the street-side shops. The real magic was inside. The building was originally known as the Westmoreland Theatre Building, and at first, the theater took the same name. Back then, the Westmoreland was more vaudeville house than movie palace. Cinema houses were still new, and audiences expected to see live performances alongside movies. But by 1939, vaudeville was passé. That year, the owners made it exclusively a movie theater, and at the same time, they rechristened it the "Waldo Theatre."

The theater's interior was ornate, but far different from the gilded palaces to be found in downtown Kansas City. Some sources report that

The original Waldo Theatre Building at Seventy-fifth and Washington Streets, circa 1930. *Betty Tillotson.*

the theater was the design of the Boller Brothers, Kansas City architects renowned for their work in movie theater design. Boller theater designs typically combined elements of Southwestern motifs and art deco angularity, and those features were present in the Waldo Theatre. Dark ceiling trusses and intricate geometric designs in bold colors were perfectly set off by the stark stucco walls. The house accommodated more than one thousand seats. Over the years, the Waldo Theatre proudly announced the opening of all the most popular films of each successive generation. Originally independently operated, it became part of Kansas City's own Commonwealth Amusement chain in 1955, which continued to operate the theater for nearly twenty years.

There is some irony to the fact that a large reason for the demise of the Waldo Theatre could be found in a national trend that had started just beyond Waldo's borders. In 1963, Kansas City's other major theater chain, the Durwood Theatres (later known as AMC Theatres) opened the nation's first multiplex movie theater at Ward Parkway Shopping Center, at Waldo's southwest corner. The shopping center had been a retail competitor of Waldo's since it opened in 1959. The Parkway Twin opened with two screens in 1963, expanded to four in 1966, and by 1969 was showing six different features simultaneously, all at relatively the same operating expense it took to run one movie at the Waldo Theatre. The competition was too stiff, and the Waldo Theatre closed forever as a movie house in 1972. In 1973, the building was sold to the Botwin family.

The building wasn't idle for long. The same year the movie theater closed, two young and eager theatrical producers, Richard Carrothers and Dennis Hennessey, were renovating an old laundry in the neighborhood just south of the Country Club Plaza into a different sort of theater. They were calling it "Tiffany's Attic Dinner Playhouse." Dinner theater was a new phenomenon in the world of stage productions. There had always been combinations of live shows with food and drink, but the dinner theater trend of the 1970s was different. The plays were light and entertaining, more in the vein of modern farce than classic drama. The comedies of Neil Simon were popular choices, as were small-scale musicals. The talent was largely local, the best of the area's professional theater troupes, but often productions were headlined by a "name"—some familiar character actor or former child star from television or film. The productions were marketed to families and groups looking for a different sort of experience, and the casual atmosphere made a night to the theater seem accessible to folks who would normally never think of going.

Carrothers and Hennessey's success with Tiffany's Attic was strong from the start. It convinced them there was room in the Kansas City market for a second venue. The old Waldo Theatre seemed like the perfect place. By some reports, the partnership invested $750,000 in the old Waldo theater space. Significant changes were needed to make the stage work for live performances. The theater entrance was reoriented to Washington Street, and the lobby motif was pure Hollywood glamour. Carrothers and Hennessey called their new place the "Waldo Astoria."

For the next seventeen years, the Waldo Astoria entertained audiences. For several years in the late 1970s, the Waldo Area Business Association and the Lions Club would buy out the house for a fundraiser night for the two organizations. All together, ninety-eight productions were mounted during the Waldo Astoria's tenure. Nationally, the dinner theater craze had come and gone, but locally, Carrothers and Hennessey had continued success with both of their theaters. Still, times were changing. The typical audience member lived south and west of Waldo and South Plaza. The aging buildings themselves offered challenges and were extraordinarily expensive to maintain. The partners had long ago incorporated their two operations into Dinner Playhouse, Inc., and over the years had moved away from involvement in daily operations. In fact, much of their work in the 1980s was outside of Kansas City, producing television and film projects. When they returned to Kansas City in 1990, they felt it was time for a change.

In April 1991, the curtain came down on the last performance of the musical comedy *Nunsense*, the final dinner theater production at the Waldo Astoria. Dinner Playhouse, Inc. was moving to Overland Park, Kansas with a new name—the New Theatre Restaurant. But the space in Waldo was still a viable theater. For a while, different performance groups and entertainment producers tried to make a go of the old theater space. But there were always issues. Complaints abounded in the neighborhood over noise and parking. The building continued to need work. In 1995, the space that had housed the once-spectacular interior of the Waldo Theatre was torn down. The lobby area was retained and converted into commercial space. But where once the auditorium had stood was a parking lot. Over the next fifteen years, the original building returned to more familiar uses. Shops and bars were at street level and offices upstairs. The bars, most recently a local Irish pub known as Kennedy's Bar & Grill, became familiar Waldo haunts. The offices and shops that filled the space were important additions to the business community. But the beautiful brick building at the corner of Seventy-fifth Street and Washington was a ghost of its former self, just another in a row of serviceable but unexceptional commercial buildings built in the 1920s.

All that changed suddenly and dramatically in February 2007. On a cold and dull winter morning, the smoke that had been smoldering for hours inside the old building was nothing more than a thin haze inside the bakery. Café Appanaire was the latest tenant of the old theater lobby space. The bakery had several ovens, so a little smoke wasn't unheard of. But this morning, the ovens weren't on. Still, the bakery workers smelled smoke. They stepped outside and heard an alarm ringing inside Kennedy's, just on the other side of the adjoining wall. It was almost ten o'clock when the first emergency calls came in. By the time firefighters reached the building only moments later, the smoke had started to billow from every crack in the old brick structure. Searching for the source of the flames, the firefighters headed into Kennedy's to find a staircase that would lead them to the second floor. It was 10:10 a.m. The only lucky break that day was that they never found those stairs.

After the Waldo Astoria closed in 1991, the theater space was temporarily a home for other productions, including Theatre for Young America. *Missouri Valley Special Collections, Kansas City Public Library, Kansas City, MO.*

Eventually, investigators would estimate the fire likely started around midnight the night before, inside a wall at Kennedy's. All night it burned at an ember's pace, causing heat and smoke to slowly build. When the firefighters arrived, they saw no flames. Figuring the fire was on the second floor, they entered the bar. What happened next was a flashover—the wild combustion that occurs when a smoldering fire has consumed all the oxygen in a closed space and is suddenly invigorated. When the firefighters came in, the air fueled the blaze. Suddenly, the building was engulfed. Five of the firefighters were caught in the inferno. They suffered injuries ranging from burns to smoke inhalation, but no lives were lost. The building, sadly, was a complete loss. The fire destroyed several businesses, including a travel agency and a bridal shop. It took several days before the few remaining charred walls of the building could be torn down, the scrap hauled away and the streets finally cleared and reopened. By then, the building's owner was already moving forward with a plan.

The family that had purchased the building forty years earlier still owned it, albeit passed to the next generation. Diane Botwin owned and managed several properties in Waldo for Botwin Development, most of them directly in the center of Waldo at Seventy-fifth Street and Wornall Road. She had recently completed a renovation of the Westmoreland Building at Seventy-fifth Street and Broadway, one of Waldo's earliest and most recognizable commercial landmarks. Botwin understood what the theater building had meant to the community and understood, too, the traditions that were important to Waldo. Yet the decision she made about the old theater building site was anything but traditional.

Botwin Commercial Development had already been in a successful working partnership with eldorado Architects, a Kansas City firm that was just becoming well known, gaining recognition as innovators in design. The firm's principals contacted Botwin before the embers had cooled and offered their support. Together, they created a visionary project. Understanding how important it was to dress the wound the fire had created, they successfully designed, financed, built and opened the new Botwin Building only eighteen months after the fire.

Waldo had never seen anything like the Botwin Building. The traditional brick exterior was gone, replaced by gleaming, art-filled glass

The Botwin Building replaced the old Waldo Theatre building after it was lost to a fire in 2007. Photograph by Mike Sinclair. *Diane Botwin/Botwin Development.*

and polished steel panels. The design was open, airy, clean and innovative. The eldorado firm was skilled at using cutting-edge techniques, and in the Botwin Building, those skills were apparent. The design incorporated natural ventilation, a central breezeway, art incorporated into the second floor windows that screened the sun and a planted roof to offset rainwater runoff.

Some worried if the Waldo community would embrace the new design. There was no need to worry. In the way Waldo seems to have always done, it adapted to the times and saw the new development as a statement that Waldo was a place in which to invest. As far as those in Waldo were concerned, as long as the Botwin Building served the community as its predecessor had, its form was irrelevant. And serve the community it did. The building had space for all the former tenants who wanted to return. Some of them had moved on, but many signed up, including Kennedy's Bar and Grill. Even in the face of innovation, Waldo traditions like a neighborhood bar will abide.

Tapped into Waldo—Betty Tillotson's Studio of Dance

In places where the sense of community is as strong as it is in Waldo, there are invariably people whose lives and careers are so aligned with that history that they become a part of the rhythm of the community. In Waldo, there is no greater example of that connection than the story of Betty Tillotson and her Studio of Dance.

Betty's story started in 1945 with a tiny advertisement in the real estate section of the newspaper. "House for Sale in Waldo area," it offered. The house was on the east side of the 7600 block of Madison Avenue. The Tillotson family knew the area well. From their home in Kansas City, Kansas, they would regularly follow the bus and streetcar connections to Waldo. Mr. Tillotson raised Scotch terriers, and the local chapter of the American Kennel Club held regular shows at the Meadow Lake Country Club at Seventy-fifth and State Line Road. The Tillotsons, including their only child, Betty, would walk by Madison on their way to the shows from the Waldo streetcar stop. Mr. Tillotson had recently taken a job at the new Pratt & Whitney plant near Ninety-fifth Street and

Troost Avenue. A home in Waldo would be much more convenient. The Tillotsons already liked the area.

When they saw the small brick house, it was love at first sight for all of them. The house was modest, but just right in every way, from the lovely gabled roof to the front room with its fireplace, to the elm trees that canopied the street. They saw it on a Saturday and wanted to buy it right away. But there was no chance to talk to the banker until Monday morning. Could the real estate agent hold it for them until then? She asked them, "How much can you put down in good faith?" Mr. Tillotson gave her all he had in his wallet—ten dollars. It was enough. On Monday, the Tillotsons had a new house.

Living in Waldo meant a shorter ride for Mr. Tillotson, but a longer one for Betty, who was finishing up her course work at Park University in Parkville. She didn't mind. She had friends to ride over with, and she loved living in Waldo from the start. She was twenty-two, and her life was filled with interests that kept her busy. She studied two of those interests—history and languages—at college. And in between times, there was dance.

Betty had been dancing since she was four. Betty and her friends were playing in the front yard when a woman came to the door of her house and asked her mother if she thought her daughter might like to take dance lessons. Betty started dancing and never stopped. By the time she moved to Waldo, she had already been a teacher and a professional dancer for several years. She performed with her dance company at local trade shows and conventions. When the war came, she performed with USO tours all around the Midwest. Often, the troupe would perform for the swing shifts at places like the Boeing plant in Wichita or Whiteman Air Force base near Knob Noster, Missouri, dancing at 3:00 a.m. She earned two dollars a show.

At home, Betty had started teaching a few neighborhood children out of her home. Mothers would approach her about their daughters. "Won't you teach my little Susie to dance? She's so clumsy." Betty loved to teach and had thought as she was attending college at Park University that she might become a grade school teacher. Teaching dance allowed her to combine the two interests and provided a little income. Since her graduation from Park University in 1947, she had been working as a secretary for a downtown insurance company.

After the move to Waldo, Betty took up where she had left off. When women of Waldo learned that Betty had taught dance, they came with pleas to help their shy or awkward children. Betty never turned them away. As she had done in Kansas City, Kansas, Betty taught on Saturdays in the front room of the family home. Her father would roll up the rug, exposing the hardwood floors. Her mother played the piano. Soon, the dance classes outgrew the front room. Then, they outgrew a neighbor's basement, and finally they outgrew the VFW Hall near Seventy-seventh Street and Wornall Road. Betty's father, who had always been her staunchest supporter and chief carpenter when it came to building sets for recitals and programs, offered a solution. He built an addition to their home, complete with all the trappings of a real dance studio.

By 1951, Tillotson had enough students for a real recital. The first recital was held on the stage of the Waldo Theatre at Seventy-fifth Street and Washington Avenue, a far cry from the cramped performances they had been giving in her home studio. The recital was a local hit and would soon become a Waldo tradition. In time, teaching from her home proved too confining for Tillotson. The constant throng of youngsters in and out of the studio became too much for the neighborhood. In 1963, Betty went looking for a more permanent home. Hoping to find a Waldo storefront to lease, she was discouraged to find that no property owner would rent to her. Some suggested she consider a location outside Waldo, but Betty would have none of it. By now, her loyalty to Waldo was firmly set. She had lived in the neighborhood, in the same house on Madison, for more than fifteen years. She was a long-standing member of Waldo's original church, Broadway Methodist on Wornall Road. She wanted to keep her studio in the heart of Waldo. Even a location at Eighty-fifth Street seemed too remote. Then she found Treasure Antiques, a small shop in the 7200 block of Wornall Road with a basement she could use. A lease was signed, and the Betty Tillotson Studio of Dance opened its doors.

Three years later, the studio was a thriving business. Tillotson relocated again to the Waldo Mart Shopping Center at Seventy-fifth Street and Wornall Road. By now, there were several dance studios in the area, serving the growing population of youngsters in the 1960s. The Betty Tillotson Studio of Dance was considered among the finest. Betty expanded her classes to include adults. Some were older students pursuing a professional career, but most came simply for the exercise and the social interaction. They came from all over the metro, but at the core were the Waldo regulars.

After more than twenty years in Waldo, Betty began to pursue another passion—her interest in the history of Waldo. Over the years, she spent much of her free time learning all she could about the area's early

Students of Betty Tillotson's Studio of the Dance have long been frequent performers at Waldo area events, such as this maypole dance from the 1970s. *Betty Tillotson.*

founders. She noted with care all the places in Waldo that were historically and culturally significant. She gathered newspaper clippings, anecdotes and photos, including those of her own students' performances. When development threatened Waldo's landmarks, she was there to advocate for preservation. She became Waldo's unofficial historian and wrote occasional articles for the area's newspapers. Betty Tillotson became the go-to person for anyone interested in Waldo's history.

As the years went by, Tillotson continued teaching. By now, she was teaching the children and grandchildren of her original students, leading them to local and national-level performances. Betty Tillotson founded the Kansas City Tap and Musical Comedy Dance Company, an adult dance group that performs and celebrates dance in the great theatrical tradition. She continued to increase her involvement in Waldo, eventually serving on the board of the business association and incorporating dance performances into events the organization sponsored. In 2000, Tillotson's interest in Waldo culminated in the publication of *The History of Waldo*, a chapbook that brought together all she had learned over the years. In

Betty Tillotson stands outside the current location of her Studio of the Dance on Gregory Boulevard, where the trophies from her many students' competitions are proudly displayed. *Betty Tillotson.*

2005, after forty years at the Waldo Mart location, Tillotson relocated her studio to Gregory Boulevard. She wasn't about to leave Waldo.

That same year, she finally sold the family house on Madison, having lived there for sixty years. It was a difficult decision, but it was time. The next year, at the annual Waldo Fall Festival, Betty was preparing her students for their performance. For several years, the program has featured the "Tap-A-Thon," where anyone with tap experience is invited to participate in a community chorus line. The "Tap-a-Thon" has become a signature piece of the annual Fall Festival. As she stood there, a young man approached her, pushing a toddler in a stroller. He asked if she was Betty Tillotson. "My wife and I bought your house," the young man said. "We just love it." For Tillotson, nothing could have brought more satisfaction than knowing someone else would come to know Waldo as she had, from the small brick house on Madison where her life-long love of Waldo began.

In 2010, Betty Tillotson celebrated sixty years of teaching dance in Waldo. That same year, she was elected Honorary Mayor of Waldo in the annual fund-raiser election held by the Waldo Area Business Association. The election was appropriate, but in one sense almost superfluous. Betty Tillotson had already been Waldo's best ambassador for most of her life.

WALDO'S NOTABLES

Over the years, Waldo has been home to noteworthy people. These distinguished Waldonians have played their part in shining a light on the place they called home—at one time or another.

Calvin Trillin

Calvin Trillin is one of America's most highly regarded and beloved men of letters. Born in 1935 in Kansas City, Trillin was raised in Waldo and is a graduate of Southwest High School. His father, Abe Trillin, operated several area grocery stores in the 1930s and '40s and later ran Trillin's Restaurant at 201 East Gregory Boulevard. Calvin Trillin attended Yale University, where he graduated in 1957. Over his writing and publishing career, he has served

In 1940, the building at Gregory Boulevard and Grand Avenue was new. In the 1950s, it would be home to Trillin's Restaurant, operated by the father of noted author Calvin Trillin. *Kansas City (MO) Landmarks Commission.*

as a staff writer for many national magazines including *Time*, the *Nation* and the *New Yorker*. His writings have spanned a range of topics and tones. For more than twenty years, Trillin has authored books on food, politics, poetry, memoir and fiction. His 1997 book, *Messages from My Father*, recounts many of his experiences growing up in the Waldo area.

Frederic James

Artist Frederic James was born in Kansas City in 1915. Displaying his talent for painting at an early age, Kansas City's Nelson-Atkins Museum of Art included one of his watercolors for exhibition in 1934. Though he was trained in architecture at the Cranbrook Academy of Art in Michigan (where he became close friends with Aero Saarinen and Charles Eames), painting was his passion. In 1939, he returned to Kansas City from Cranbrook to teach at the Kansas City Art Institute. Like his good friend and contemporary Thomas Hart Benton, James is associated with the Regionalist art movement. He enlisted in the army during World War

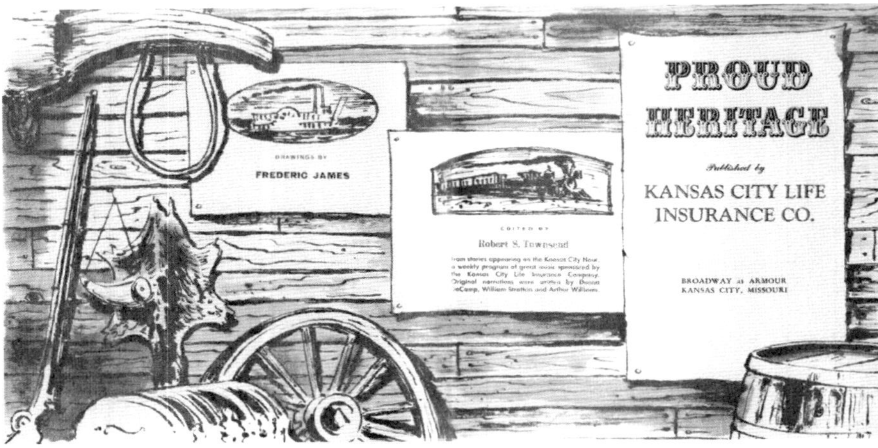

Nationally acclaimed artist and Kansas City native Frederic James was a resident of Waldo when he produced illustrations for this promotional piece on Kansas City's history in 1957. *LaDene Morton.*

II and, afterward, returned to Kansas City yet again, this time taking up residence in Waldo with his new wife. From this point to the end of his life in 1985, James concentrated strictly on his own work, producing award-winning and nationally recognized watercolors, taking inspiration from the rural landscapes of Missouri and Kansas.

H. Roe Bartle

Among the list of notable people who have served as mayor of Kansas City, Missouri, none have been more popular or more well-regarded than H. Roe Bartle. Born in 1896 in Virginia, Harold Roe Bartle first came to Missouri in 1923 where his father was a minister. Even before that, Bartle had become involved in a fledgling organization known as the Boy Scouts. Scouting would be a lifelong passion, and in 1928, he became Kansas City's chief area executive for the organization. It was there he earned the nickname "the Chief," a name that would stay with him his entire life and a name that served as the inspiration for the Kansas City football team's mascot. Scouting at the executive level, along with his law degree, fostered an interest in civic affairs. He was near retirement age when, in 1955, he successfully ran for mayor. He served until 1963 and, for the following eleven years, remained civically active and involved with scouting. He died in 1974 and remains fondly remembered for his larger-than-life personality, his gift for oratory and his national influence with the Boy Scouts of America. Bartle and his wife Margaret lived for most of his career on East Seventieth Street in Waldo.

BIBLIOGRAPHY

The following materials provided a rich context for the understanding of Waldo's own history, as well as its place in both the history of Kansas City and in the changing times of the twentieth century.

Articles

Bodine, Walt. "The Good, the Bad and The Ugly." *Town Squire*, March 1974.

Boulevard Magazine. "Waldo Hysteria." July 1984.

Bryan, Craig M. "Before Electric Park: A Promenade of Early Kansas City Area Amusement Parks." *Jackson County Historical Society JOURNAL*, Spring 2006.

City Ice Man. "Waldo, a Beautiful City of Homes." April 1925.

Dvorak, John A. "Winding Fight for Track Rights." *Kansas City Times*, November 5, 1977.

Kansas City Star. "Abandoned Water Tower Yields Body." August 1962.

———. "Civil War! Sesquecentennial Special Edition." April 10, 2011.

———. "Loss of Rock Barn Leaves Mysteries." December 17, 1997.

———. "Waldo History—Community Enterprise." August 17, 1947.

Leathers, Tom. "They Couldn't Tear it Down…Could They?" *Squire*, April 17, 1980.

Leifer, Loring. "The Napoleon of Southtown." *SouthTown News Magazine*, July 1985.

McPherron, Till. "Famous Majors Home Faces an Uncertain Future." *Jackson County Historical Society JOURNAL*, October 1961.

New York Times. "Alexander Majors Dead." January 16, 1900.

Ragan, Mrs. Greenberry. "A Panoramic View of the "Lost Townships." *Jackson County Historical Society JOURNAL*, July and December, 1965.

Samuel, T.D. Jr., "Concrete Standpipe for 110 Ft. Heat at Kansas City." *Engineering News-Records*, October 28, 1920.

Sloan, Waldo Douglas. "Dr. David Waldo—Physician, Soldier, Santa Fe Trader and Big Landholder." *Jackson County Historical Society JOURNAL*, Spring 1968.

SouthTown News Magazine. "Waldo Cleans Up Its Act." July 1985.

Squire. "Toeing the Line." September 27, 1979.

———. "What is Waldo's Secret?" October 21, 1971.

Town Magazine. "Do You Know Kansas City?" October 3, 1947.

Turner, Paul. "The Old Dummy Line from Westport to Waldo." *Westport Historical Quarterly* 5, no. 1 (June 1969).

Umland, Rudoph. "Waldo: The Man Behind It." *City Window*, February/March 1974.

Wednesday Magazine. "Waldo 1907." October 17, 1969.

Westport Sentinel Examiner. "Tapped." December 22, 1894.

———. "Waldo Land and Investment Co." (advertisement). May 11, 1895.

———. "Westport and Waldo Railway." March 24, 1894.

Wornall, Mrs. John B. "Account of the Battle of Westport and Early Memories of Kansas City." *Jackson County Historical Society JOURNAL*, October 1961.

BOOKS

Burke, Diane Mutti and John Herron, eds. *Kansas City, America's Crossroads: Essays from the Missouri Historical Review, 1906-2006*. Columbia: State Historical Society of Missouri, 2007.

Conrad, Howard L. *Encyclopedia of the History of Missouri*. New York: Southern History Company, 1901.

DeAngelo, Dory. *What About Kansas City! A Historical Handbook*. Kansas City: Two Lane Press, Inc., 1995.

Dodd, Monroe. *A Spendid Ride: The Streetcars of Kansas City 1870–1950*. Kansas City: Kansas City Star Books, 2002.

Garwood, Darrell. *Crossroads of America: The Story of Kansas City*. New York: W.W. Norton & Company, Inc., 1948.

Green, George Fuller. *A Condensed History of the Kansas City Area: Its Mayors and some VIPs*. Kansas City: The Lowell Press, 1968.

Gregg, Josiah. *The Commerce of the Prairies.* New York: Henry G. Langley Publishing, 1859.

Haskell, Henry C. Jr. and Fowler, Richard B. *City of the Future: The Story of Kansas City 1850–1950*. Kansas City: Frank Glenn Publishing Co., Inc., 1950.

History of Jackson County, Missouri. Union Historical Company, 1881.

Jackson, David W. *Kansas City Chronicles: An Up-to-Date History*. Charleston: The History Press, 2010.

Kirkman, Paul. *The Battle of Westport*. Charleston: The History Press, 2011.

Majors, Alexander. *Seventy Years on the Frontier.* Chicago: Rand McNally & Company, 1893.

McAlester, Virginia and Lee. *A Field Guide to American Houses*. New York: Alfred A. Knopf, 1986.

McCandless, Perry. *A History of Missouri: Volume II 1820-1860*. Columbia: University of Missouri Press, 1971, 2000.

Montgomery, Rick and Shiel Kasper. *Kansas City: An American Story*. Kansas City: Kansas City Star Books, 1999.

Trillin, Calvin. *Messages from My Father*. New York: Farrah, Straus and Giroux, 1996.

Wilborn, Chris. *Where the Streetcar Stops.* Kansas City: Wilborn & Associates Photographers, 1991.

Wilkerson, Jami. *Path to Glory: A Pictorial Celebration of the Santa Fe Trail.* Kansas City: Highwater Editions, 1996.

Winther, Oscar O. *The Transportation Frontier.* New York: Holt, Rinehart and Winston, 1964.

Worley, Dr. William S. *J.C. Nichols and the Shaping of Kansas City*. Columbia and London: University of Missouri Press, 1990.

Public Reports, Pamphlets, Chapbooks and Brochures

A Story on the Development of the Parks and Recreation Department (published on the occasion of its Diamond Jubilee 1892–1967). Kansas City, Missouri Parks and Recreation Commission, 1967.

Bruce, Janet. "The John Wornall House 1858." Jackson County Historical Society.

Haskell, Harry. "City of the Future: Kansas City's Progressive Utopia." Charles N. Kimball Lecture Series, Western Historical Manuscript Collection, Kansas City, April 10, 2008.

"Proud Heritage." Kansas City: Kansas City Life Insurance Co., 1957.

Results of County Planning. Jackson County, Missouri, 1932.

Slater, William A. "What We Do Best is Care." Kansas City: Women's Christian Association, 1995.

Tillotson, Betty. "A History of Waldo." Almar Printing, 2000.

Treanor Architects. "Waldo Water Tower: Condition Assessment Report." August 25, 2010.

ATLASES AND MAPS

Atlas, Kansas City, Missouri and Environs, 1925. Tuttle, Ayers, Woodward.

Atlas of the City of Kansas City, Jackson County, Missouri. Hottelmann, 1881.

Beck, Warren A., and Ynez D. Haase, eds. *Historical Atlas of the American West.* Norman: University of Oklahoma Press, 1989.

Illustrated Atlas of Jackson County, Missouri, 1877. Jackson County Historical Society (centennial reprint, 1977.)

Plat Book of Jackson County, Missouri, 1904. Northwest Publishing Co.

Plat Book of Jackson County, Missouri, 1911. Berry Publishing co.

Residential Developments in Metropolitan Kansas City by the J.C. Nichols Company (map and promotional brochure). J.C. Nichols Company, 1967.

Sanborn Fire Insurance Maps, 1939–1958, Sanborn Map Company.

INDEX

P

R

S

T

U

V

W

ABOUT THE AUTHOR

LaDene Morton holds a masters in public administration from the University of Kansas and has studied and practiced community and economic development for more than thirty years in areas all across the United States. She is a former resident of the Waldo area, where she also operated her professional practice for ten years. She is the author of *The Brookside Story: Shops of Every Necessary Character* and has authored one work of fiction, *What Lies West*, a historical novel about the American West.

Visit us at
www.historypress.net